What CEOs Need to Know:

The #1 Reason Startups Fail and <u>All</u> Organizations Underperform

ISBN: 978-1-956257-19-9

Cover Photo Credit #190631738 3Dgenerator dreamstime.com

The greatest danger in times of turbulence is not the turbulence; it is to act with yesterday's logic."
— Peter Drucker

Contents

WARNING!

"There is nothing in a caterpillar that tells you it's going to be a butterfly."

— R. Buckminster Fuller

Dear Reader,

What you are about to read is not always going to feel comfortable. This is a transformative book, and just like a caterpillar transforms into a butterfly, you can quickly and easily transform your organization from status quo to a Wildly Successful Enterprise. Your organization can move faster and fly higher than you thought possible – *reach its maximum potential* - but as a leader you must be willing to take on the less familiar to get there.

Because you have taken the leap of leading an organization or starting your own, you understand that sometimes we must get uncomfortable before we have our greatest triumphs. I am going to take you out of the environment in which you have been comfortable - to help you realize that you are stuck in an old paradigm and then present reasoning to *accept a new paradigm*. You will begin, one-by-one, to reject all the status quo business and organizational practices that have kept you stuck.

I wanted to let you know that if it hurts your ego a little bit, if it is difficult to realize the pain traditional practices create, you are doing it right. Feeling the pain means you are open, means you are receiving, means you are listening, and that means that you have potential, that you can accept a new and effective organizational model. I promise it is going to be worth it if you can find the humility to change practices that are not working for you, your customers, or your employees. On the other side of that realization is prosperity, and most importantly, joy.

And that is why I wanted to stop you before you read this book and let you know; it is okay if it feels uncomfortable. Provided it feels uncomfortable enough that you want to give me a call, you can book a 15-minute Insights call with me by visiting wildlysuccessfulenterprises.com.

Together, we can create a new future of working together!

All the best,

Dawn Holly

ACKNOWLEDGEMENTS

To my daughters Moorea and Tasha: For dealing with an overworked mother constantly caught in professional crossfire and sometimes so disillusioned she could not always be present. For dealing with so much moving and change while I constantly had to switch gears to support us. We experienced a less than stable home life and livelihood, and I believe navigating these challenges made us all stronger - and was not without sacrifice. For my being absorbed most every evening working on this book during your teen and young adult years, and for you always cheering me on regardless. You are my reason this work exists and that my passion for it will never end. It all started with my desiring a better future for you.

To my sister Tara: Thank you for being my biggest admirer and loving me through the tough times.

To my stepdaughter Heather: For being a great older sister and presence for Moorea and Tasha. For seeing me as a "powerful and up-to-something woman" in your life – it has made a difference that you believe in me.

To my Great Aunt Rita: Thank you for your encouragement to start again, and your constant support while offering me a home as I pursued my engineering degree for the second go-around at the age of twenty-five and after life had beaten me down. Thank you for all you did for my mother, for our family. I miss you dearly.

To my cheerleaders Aunt Rita and Jeanette: Thank you for always believing in me and encouraging me to stay true to myself. You have both filled whatever role was necessary: mother, friend, confidant, and business and life advisor. Your positive presence in my life has meant so much, and my gratitude for you is immeasurable.

To my dear friend Lysa: Your nurturing friendship helps me laugh and find joy and faith repeatedly, even through the darkest times.

To Lloyd: For showing me what true leadership can be in a corporate setting. For being a visionary, for trusting me with much responsibility at such a youthful age and empowering me to bring my talents for positive change.

To Dan, Jeremy, and Lori: For reviewing manuscripts to ensure the most powerful message was present to the reader of this book. Thank you for your dedication to The Future of Working Together.

To Jacquie and Sharla: For coaching me through the challenging times and making sure I celebrated the good and held my faith in me.

To Kyle: Thank you for being a model of transcending the status quo.

To the many wonderful friends and family who pre-read the book at differing times of its development and supplied valuable feedback. Thank you for your generosity and love.

To Mom and Dad: You taught me and Tara an amazing work ethic – to work hard and work smart. You taught me to take something and design it to work and be beautiful and practical, experience that has paid off professionally and personally for my entire life. Tara and I lost you both too soon, but your strengths live on in us.

To you, the reader, for taking on a new future – now make it count!

FOREWORD

I began drafting this book in 2016, an exceedingly difficult year for me both personally and professionally. I had experienced many challenging times in the past, but this was different. Leaders were threatening my livelihood, my family's welfare, as I was working to make their teams successful. As I began to ask new questions, I began to realize and understand a new concept. Seeing the world newly means we never see the world in the same way ever again. Once I realized an empowering solution to how we can work together in harmony, I no longer tolerate the old.

For over two decades now, I have been able to recognize the problems created from status quo thinking and the hardship of working in traditional organizations. I was one of those experiencing that hardship. There had to be a better way. It is difficult to watch traditional organizations do what they do. I have taken several hiatus' from writing over the years, waiting to publish until now, as I believe there is enough societal momentum to support the evolution of value focused organizations.

INTEGRITY. DETERMINATION. PURPOSE.

"I want to be thoroughly used up when I die, for the harder I work, the more I live. I rejoice in life for its own sake. Life is no 'brief candle' to me. It is sort of a splendid torch which I have a hold of for the moment, and I want to make it burn as brightly as possible before handing it over to future generations."

- George Bernard Shaw

I was born in Calgary, Canada to parents raised on farms. This presented me with opportunities for growth and development to perform many advanced tasks for my age. My parents never gave me the impression that I could not do something because I was a girl. From the time I was three years old, my parents would buy a house, we would live in it, renovate it, and move to the next one. By the age of fourteen, I knew how to frame, plumb, wire, and drywall a house, build a fence, and shingle a roof, perform basic car repairs and maintenance, paint, sew, and cook. After taking aptitude tests at age 14, I chose to pursue a career in engineering. By age 17, I had matriculated into the University of Calgary Engineering Program. I walked into my first class and into a sea of men. Three hundred men and Calculus and me.

So what? I live in a world where I can take on anything if I put my all into it.

Mom had become extremely ill by then. Dad was in the oil & gas exploration business, and my sister and I moved with him to Denver after I completed my first year of university. Mom stayed in Canada. My sister was only eleven when we arrived in Denver and Dad traveled a lot. I took one more year of studies at the University of Colorado at Boulder in Electrical Engineering. I was a guardian for my sister and traveling to Canada on breaks to take care of Mom. It was all too overwhelming. So, I quit school.

From the age of thirteen, I had already pursued various blue-collar roles: I had been a great newspaper girl, daycare worker, landscaper, seismic geophone repairer, and cocktail server. I would take on anything – I love to learn. I brought all the competence I could to everything I did. If I could not do it well, then why do it?

INTEGRITY.

Mom died two years after I quit college. Then I disappeared for two more – I do not remember much from that time, although I did become a cosmetologist – a profession where I could have flexible work hours to be home for my sister. I awoke one day and realized I was rudderless. My focus had been on taking care of others and I had forgotten about myself. My sister was about to turn eighteen, and so I decided to move back to Canada to restart my life. My great aunt offered to put a roof over my head if I would just go back to school. I had to start all over – it had been six years since my last collegiate class.

So, I started over. Onto the pursuit of something better.

My plan had been to travel the world after getting my degree at 21, but those dreams would have to wait. I wanted and needed that engineering degree. For me.

Two years later I had an Associates in Engineering but could not find the desire to transfer back to the University of Calgary. Too many painful memories. So, I moved to Phoenix, Arizona, USA where I could afford to live and attend university full time. My sister followed me a few years later. We both have Canadian and US citizenship. I had three more years of study to go, due to lost credits from transferring to yet another university in another country.

During those final three summers at college, I took on internships at two of the largest oil companies in Canada. I had the chance to travel to the Arctic and follow in my old man's footsteps. By my senior year, I had already generated twenty million in new revenue for those companies.

I had worked my way through four universities across two countries, seven years of study with $40,000 in loans over a span of 13 years. I graduated cum laude at 30 years of age. Family and friends came from all over North America to see me walk on graduation day. I had the biggest cheering section at Arizona State University. My sister surprised me with a big banner that declared "Way to Go Dawny, We Love You!" (I still have it) and it took everyone to hold it up. On the top of my graduation cap, I had glued the letters "Hi Mom!" in gold sparkle to match my burgundy and gold ensemble. My sister told me later that dad broke down when I walked out.

No one was prouder of me that day, than me. Nobody.

Through all adversity, I had stuck it out. I was my word. That is integrity. DETERMINATION.

I was the only one of my graduating class with a job waiting for me. I had fought for that too. Working for a premiere aerospace company, I learned Total Quality Management and Lean Six Sigma. For seven years I pursued developing myself not as a typical engineer, but as one that engineers organizations to be effective and efficient.

In 2001, Dad suffered a massive stroke at age 66 due to medical error. Time to take care of parent number two. I was married, the main breadwinner, and had two girls ages 1 and 5. Dad lingered for five long years. We never sued the Doctor; he had learned his lesson. But I did some research and discovered Medical Error is the third leading cause of death in the United States, and those numbers are under-reported. I became determined to improve the healthcare system. It was a broken system that killed my father - a broken process without accountability to proven standards – something that would not have happened easily in aerospace. Both aerospace and healthcare are life and death industries – why does one have a far higher safety record than the other? Engineering.

Over the next eight years, persecuted for offering proven changes that felt threatening to leaders working in immature organizational systems – systems that were 50 years behind manufacturing - I experienced how far behind service and transactional companies are as compared to manufacturing.

I pursued a business transformation role in higher education for a needed culture change. Weak systems and processes prevailed again. I began to wonder how we as a race had survived this long. Frequent layoffs eventually degraded my marriage and our finances, and my ex-husband and I divorced in 2016, with me taking on all the debt from the marriage.

I lost my job a week later. I could not find work - a contract – anything - for 14 months. It was an US election year, and the country was torn apart, and I was a single parent with two teenage girls to support, with only $70,000 in retirement and $40,000 in debt. I partnered in three startups, with each CEO touting my capabilities to investors and then not following my recommendations. All three startups, which had brilliant potential, failed.

By the start of 2017 I did not have money. I landed a role in telecommunications just in time to make rent. Another total mess. Then banking. Same messes. More layoffs.

By now, I had contributed over $6 Billion in value creation without much appreciation for my efforts. I had to figure out why there was so much resistance to creating healthy organizations.

I started drafting a book.

Through this cathartic effort of writing, my frustration was with leaders I had worked with who refused to improve the health of their organizations, and yet prevailed. I had to start asking myself new questions. What is it that they do not see? Then I figured it out. I call this my big AH-HA moment.

As I was writing, I realized something quite profound. If my career had not constantly forced me to pursue roles in different industries and organizations I would not have progressed in my knowledge and experience so quickly. I would not have experienced working in every industry, in every size organization, with the purview of an organizational designer and value creator and honed my engineering mind to solve these systemic issues. This unique combination of training and experience has enabled me to see what holds us back from creating a powerful future of working together.

Every organization on the planet is underperforming compared to its maximum potential. There is no denying it. We need to design and engineer organizations for high performance. If every organization on earth delivered value both effectively and efficiently, no human being on the planet would go without their basic needs met. Not one. I had found my...

PURPOSE.

Now this book, What CEOs Need to Know, and the Wildly Successful Enterprises Program^{SM} exist, both aimed at quickly transforming any organization into a productive, collaborative, future-ready environment designed to achieve unprecedented results.

Most of the workforce is suffering. Time to end the suffering.

INTEGRITY. DETERMINATION. PURPOSE.

These are the core values that I choose to live by. Choose to Be Authentic – to be your best self.

YOU are all you can ever really count on.

We can change the future...The Future of Working Together - for the betterment of all.

Thank you for reading.

INTRODUCTION

What CEOs Need to Know

"Here's to the crazy ones, the misfits, the rebels, the troublemakers, the round pegs in the square holes ... the ones who see things differently -- they're not fond of rules, and they have no respect for the status quo. ... You can quote them, disagree with them, glorify, or vilify them, but the only thing you cannot do is ignore them because they change things. ... They push the human race forward, and while some may see them as the crazy ones, we see genius, because the people who are crazy enough to think that they can change the world, are the ones who do."

– Steve Jobs

My claim is simple and bold:

Every organization on the planet is underperforming as compared to its maximum potential.

It is our organizations – our businesses, governments, healthcare, and educational systems - that can make the greatest shift, and therefore the greatest impact in creating a workable future for us all. Historically, organizations have wasted vast amounts of resources - be they earthly, financial, or human – to the detriment of the human condition and to our planet. Imagine if every organization on the planet had a valuable purpose and was working effectively and efficiently to deliver value for the world. The result would be that no human being on the planet would go without their basic needs met. This in turn would create an environment for societies and economies to thrive – along with this beautiful planet we call home. Inherit in this vision exists the ability for everyone born to this planet to thrive. The children of the world deserve this to be so. Currently, what do we have instead? Scarcity. Politics. Suffering. Wasted resources. Ineffectiveness. We are failing ourselves.

Organizations deliver on a purpose, yet they are not designed or led to do this. We either work within an organization or interact with one or more organizations every day. **What if I told you that traditional organizations are:**

    - not focused on supplying value to you as a customer

    - not designed to make it easy for people to work together

    - not embracing a mindset to adapt, innovate, and continuously improve.

The impact of underperforming organizations is that we waste an immeasurable amount of time and energy every day to function. Please stop for a moment and reflect on your professional journey so far. Chances are you have spent more time dealing with politics and bureaucracy than in delivering value in your professional lifetime. Now imagine creating powerful environments where people can effectively collaborate to deliver on a meaningful purpose. It is possible, and first we must understand what causes some level of dysfunction in every organization.

So, how can I dare to make the claim that every organization on the planet is underperforming?

I have accumulated 25 years of proof based on my rare professional experience and natural abilities to see patterns in what to most people is disparate information. I see ways to maximize the potential in any situation, in people and in organizations. I recognize systemic problems and look for ways to improve upon them. But do not take my word for it, the proof that organizations underperform is everywhere. Below is only a small sampling of statistics to prove the point.

According to the Gallup State of the Global Workplace report, on average over the last 10 years, only 15 percent of employees are engaged in the workplace.

In the U.S alone, disengaged employees cost organizations ~ $450-550 billion each year.

Excerpt from https://www.gallup.com/workplace/349484/state-of-the-global-workplace.aspx

A Harvard Business Review survey reveals 58 percent of people say they trust strangers more than their own boss. **We live in a world where cultural trust is at an all-time low.**

Global studies reveal that 79% of people who quit their jobs cite 'lack of appreciation' as their reason for leaving.

The Conference Board reports that 53 percent of Americans are currently unhappy at work.

U.S. workers forfeited nearly 50% of their paid vacation in 2017, with nearly 10 percent not taking any vacation time. According to a study by Glassdoor, the fear of falling behind is the number one reason people are not using their vacation time.

Excerpt from https://www.forbes.com/sites/davidsturt/2018/03/08/10-shocking-workplace-stats-you-need-to-know/

Customers will spend 17 percent more for an enjoyable experience. Customer-centric companies are 60% more profitable than companies that are not, with $1.6 trillion lost each year due to poor customer experience.

Excerpt from https://blog.hubspot.com/service/customer-experience-trends

According to a survey of over 300,000 individuals, 83% defined their workplace cultures as non-resilient, with the leading culture type being passive-aggressive at 27%.[1]

Harvard Business Review https://hbr.org/2005/10/the-passive-aggressive-organizatio

Fewer than 25% of Founding CEOs have led their companies to initial public offerings
4/5 Founders are asked to step down from CEO positions.

https://hbr.org/2008/02/the-founders-dilemm

Let us investigate how we got here.

Any practice adopted by the status quo becomes a norm in society, whether it is the right thing to do or not. In the 1950's smoking was a cultural norm, considered a healthy practice and promoted by doctors for stress relief. When finally measured, the effects of smoking were determined to be detrimental to the human body.

The detriment to society from underperforming organizations is clear in the above statistics, yet the way to stop the dysfunction in business, in any organization, is to stop applying ineffective practices. Yet, as creatures of habit, we continue to be stuck in an antiquated and ineffective paradigm. Taught the same basic approaches to run and lead an organization, we apply them - but this does not mean that they are the best approaches, and the negative impact on society is overwhelming. Depression and anxiety are on the rise as people work in fear-based cultures while trying to contribute their talents. Neither the school of hard knocks nor the top MBA programs teach what is necessary to create thriving organizations. Simply put, we do not design organizations to function at their maximum potential.

There are fourteen traditional practices I challenge in this book, and I will offer fourteen alternative practices to replace them – practices proven beneficial in eradicating common problems we experience today in organizations. The fourteen practices I recommend will accelerate positive change as you have never experienced before, and I have combined these practices into a new and simplified operating model.

Replacing a known practice with a new one is simply adopting something different.

But DIFFERENT does not mean DIFFICULT.

"All entrepreneurs deserve the greatest chance for success."
– Dawn Holly Johnson

Associates of mine call me the "six-billion-dollar woman" because I have worked to bring positive change *across every major industry and in every size of organization* resulting in over $6B in value creation to date. I derived most of that value from generating new revenue after streamlining how the business worked, which improved customer relationships and willingness to invest in new products or services. In this role, I have had the rare opportunity to assess entire organizations from a unique vantage point, enabling me to become quickly acquainted with the way an entire organization works. I always uncover large opportunities that those running the organization are unaware of. Why is it that no matter what organization I evaluate, there is dramatic opportunity for improvement? Having experienced extraordinary exposure to all types of organizations has allowed me to recognize something quite profound: That all traditional organizations, and the people working in them, are dealing with a multitude of common problems.

Always the same problems.

And no traditional organization is infallible to these problems.

Yet as I have worked to solve these common problems, I met far more resistance than acceptance towards recommended alternative practices. Why have most leaders I have worked with chosen to leave billions in opportunity, along with the chance to create a thriving organizational culture, on the table? **In asking myself this question, I worked to find the answer. This book is a result of that inquiry.**

As a business owner / leader, I am sure you do not want to leave money on the table, nor miss an opportunity to improve the health of your organization and the people working in it. As an individual contributor, I am sure you would prefer to work in a collaborative and effective environment. Rarely do I hear from people that they thoroughly enjoy working in their organization or hear that they are delighted in interacting with an organization as a customer.

Common accepted approaches to business and managing organizations merely derive from natural human tendencies and are unfortunately ineffective. Some common approaches followed today arose during the industrial revolution, where the need was to manage and control an uneducated workforce, but this is not the condition we find ourselves in today. Getting to the root cause of the matter – why there are a myriad of problems common to all organizations

– I looked for correlation of traditional practices to common problems, and from this analysis created organizational models that do not allow for these common problems to exist. With any improvements I have ever made in an organization, I have simply designed-out the ability for the problem to occur. The organizational models I will recommend here – differing for each sector - can prevent today's common business and organizational problems. Make no mistake, status quo practices are ineffective…even damaging. In fact, I will prove to you that status quo practices are nothing but unquestioned evolution.

Status quo practices are nothing but unquestioned evolution.

Regardless of the industry or the size of an organization, ask a CEO what problems they face, and they voice the same fundamental issues in any order:

1. **Creating and Sustaining Equity** – Struggling to create and ensure strong revenue streams while keeping expenses minimized.

2. **Reliable, Persistent, Healthy Cash Flow** – Not knowing real-time how well the organization is performing and exactly what to do to create reliable cash flow.

3. **Profitability** – Difficulty sustaining high performance for the organization.

4. **Alignment** – Never-ending challenges with aligning people to focus on the right things to deliver on and achieve intended results.

5. **Employee Productivity** – Creating a productive work environment.

6. **Developing Leaders** is a common struggle CEOs face.

7. **Finding and Keeping Great Talent** – Ensuring the organization is hiring the right people at the right time with the right skills is paramount yet daunting.

8. **Employee Retention** – Employee engagement is difficult to create or sustain.

9. **Accountability** - Having strong leadership and clear accountability, with meaningful performance management.

10. **Communication** – Having effective collaboration throughout the organization with clear lines of communication.

11. **Execution** - Successfully executing new strategies, products, projects, and plans.

12. **Successfully Managing Growth** - Ensuring predictable and scalable growth without creating overburden or failure to deliver.

13. **Adaptability and Innovation** - Having the organization be innovative and nimble, adaptable to a constantly changing marketplace. The recent pandemic has heightened the need for team cohesion while reducing work related stressors.

14. **Customer Acquisition and Retention** – Generating consistent revenues and growth.

15. **Customer Experience** – Improving the experience of customers interacting with the organization.

This is a long (and non-inclusive) list. Every traditional organization is dealing with these problems at some degree and in some form or fashion.

Ask employees the challenges they face, and they express the same basic stressors:

1. **Difficulty performing meaningful work and loss of productivity** – Too many meetings with nothing much accomplished or decided upon. Too many projects, diluting the ability to pay adequate attention to the daily responsibilities of their role. Constant uncontrolled changes to processes and systems. Lack of purpose.

2. **Fear of job loss** – Working in constant fear of losing one's livelihood – not because of personal underperformance, but as the fallout created

from temporary unsustainable budget cuts CEOs and CFOs enact to try to gain equity and from working with ineffective processes and systems. With each downsize, employees inherit more work and become less productive, as downsizing does nothing to improve efficiency.

3. **Confusion from reorganization** - working in a constantly changing environment that disconnects people from workflow and leaves them no longer knowing what to do, or who to go to for what. (I see reorganization as analogous to disrupting an ant trail, as once this happens, the ants lose track of where to find nourishment)

4. **Subjective arbitrary performance reviews** – People consistently measured against unattainable goals and evaluated not on what they are doing well, but on what they are not. Reviews are subjective and heavily rely on the ability of a manager to perceive the value people create. In organizations that often reorganize, a new manager that has no notion about an employee's actual prior accomplishments performs the review.

5. **Fear of speaking up** – Living in the fear of communicating work-related issues - as anything other than positive results are unaccepted by leadership. Receiving top-down communication only. Leadership disconnected from what is really happening is a big frustration for the common worker. Most workers have learned to just keep their mouth shut and stay heads down in the work, no matter how ridiculous that work is, to avoid penalty for trying to improve how the organization functions.

6. **Passive aggressive culture** – The most common culture in organizations is the behavior where individuals agree to an initiative in public and then silently resist the effort entirely. This is due to lack of accountability and elevated levels of politics, favoritism, and nepotism, leaving those that are competent but not politically astute unrecognized. The strongest and most confident people will end up leaving the organization entirely.

7. **Leadership not living cultural values** – Traditional Leadership will often promote cultural values and then not follow them, yet the worker must do so or have their performance record negatively affected.

Every organization is underperforming as compared to its maximum potential.

It is apparent that traditional practices are highly ineffective, yet they are routine - woven into the fabric of society - with the outcome of suffering. But fear not: you will learn to see a simplified view of how the world can work. Here we will focus on your entire organization to uncover the fundamental systemic flaws and societal beliefs that create common problems.

Designing an organization involves defining the purpose of the organization and then creating the systems and structures for the people in the organization to deliver on that purpose effectively and efficiently. **We should not merely form and grow organizations organically; we can *design them to work and grow effectively.***

In this age of constantly accelerating change, it is imperative to design organizations to be adaptable, productive, innovative, and collaborative. I am a woman that wants to influence a better world, now and for future generations. **Managing or working in any organization need not be so difficult, yet conventional wisdom has made it so. Yet, we can adopt an organizational model that can quickly and positively transform organizations through making basic changes in Focus, Structure, and Mindset.**

Focus

Do you have a compelling vision for your organization? How well have you communicated this with the people working in your organization? Lack of organizational alignment stems from lack of focus, poor structure, and the wrong mindset. Consistent focus on the purpose of your business is the first step in creating strong organizational alignment. Likely, everyone in your organization has a different viewpoint on the purpose of their role and that of the organization, and consequently their combined efforts are analogous to everyone in a rowboat paddling at a different cadence and in different directions.

Organizations are hard to manage, and waste vast amounts of resources (human and capital) due to lack of focus. Creating a laser focus sounds easy, but not in a traditional organization due to its very structure.

Structure

Traditional organizations share design flaws that tend to go unquestioned as our human inclination leans towards one way of organizing and managing people. Let us use a teapot as a metaphor for organizational design. One advantage of a teapot design is to hold hot water, and keep it hot, to allow the tea to steep. A second advantage of the teapot is its handle, designed so that the user does not burn their hand to move the teapot. A third advantage of teapot design is a spout that can accurately pour tea into a cup. Now, imagine if our teapot was a large, flat, wide-mouthed bowl. How hot would the water stay? How hard would it be to pick up the vessel? How well would we pour water into a cup? A well-designed teapot pours hot water infused with tea with order and elegance. Without the proper design, the proper structure, we cause a mess.

The design, or structure, of any entity decides its usefulness – this is true for organizations delivering on their purpose just as it is true for products and services.

Organizational structure dictates human behavior and how well you deliver value.

Mindset

Today's business mindset is to focus on the immediate – the current work and daily problems at hand. Cultures have become reactive and passive-aggressive instead of collaborative and productive. Continuous change, not continuous improvement, has become the name of the game. Traditional organizational focus is not to create practical systems for everyone to work within. Most people are not systems thinkers, a point I will prove later, yet people can adapt to systems easily.

An example of a system is a traffic system. When you become a driver, you learn about the system and perform a driving test. Within a brief period, the unconscious portion of our brain is able to navigate as the system is easy to follow. How often have you arrived at your destination and not remembered most of the driving journey? You did not have to design the system to understand it and follow it. But the traffic system has rules, and when we break the rules, accidents can happen. Traditionally organizational designs are like not having a traffic system to get to your destination, with accidents happening daily as little definition or enforcement of a system exists.

What CEOs need to know is how to make simple changes in organizational Focus, Structure, and Mindset to quickly evolve any organization to achieve unprecedented results in scaled growth, employee engagement and alignment, collaboration, innovation, productivity, profitability, customer experience, customer acquisition and retention, and more - all with simplified management for scalable growth, reliable cash flow, and a joyful culture. So why isn't this the norm?

It has become clear to me that when an expert proposes an alternative approach to improving organizational management and performance there is a critical gap in thinking: that expert assumes that this alternative approach is both understood and appreciated. I have come to realize that ***the very nature of traditional practices actually defies the understanding and appreciation of best practice adoption.*** Recognizing this fact was the breakthrough moment for me that ignited the writing of this book.

There are many experts touting best practices, but they do not realize that these methods conflict with status quo thinking, causing resistance to the adaptation of these practices. As a change agent, I too was falsely believing leaders would adopt alternative but proven and effective ways to manage and run their businesses for over 20 years, and this false belief left me blind to what is so. The common acceptance of traditional organizational management practices is the failure, yet these practices are prevalent in society. It is rare to find someone that has questioned the very premise of how we got here because we all live in the same paradigms.

It is imperative to understand that the very nature of traditional practices drives people to defy alternative practice adoption.

Traditional organizations lack the design to supply value – instead, we allow organizations to grow organically. Estimates claim that we waste over one trillion dollars in productivity each year worldwide. Burnout, depression and suicide, high staff turnover, and increased healthcare costs are the effects of the lack of value-driven design of organizations.

Conventional wisdom is making people sick.

But here is the good news: With simple changes to common institutional perspectives, we can come together to focus on delivering value to everyone we serve and modernize life as we know it. When enough people worldwide recognize that there is a simpler and more constructive way for us all to work together, we can achieve a tipping point to allow societal and economic transformation to begin - assuring a powerful future for us all. Every organization that intends to deliver value to the world can be a resilient one. The more people in the world that can embrace the simple one-time changes I present in this book, the better the world will be. This book is for the world, and it starts with educating CEOs, leaders, change agents, and individual contributors on what is possible.

This book is a potent no-nonsense guide to creating far more powerful futures than status quo approaches can ever deliver. My intention is for you to naturally realize how effectively we can work together; to show you how easy it can be to create Wildly Successful Enterprises^{SM}. You will come to believe that a new future is possible as I take you through a simple two-part approach:

1. I will prove how status quo / traditional / conventional practices that society has unconsciously embraced are ineffective in running organizations and detrimental to the people working in them.
2. I will recommend replacing conventional practices with timeless proven practices that will enhance all areas of performance while improving the experience of the people engaging with, and working within, an organization.

In this two-part approach we address organizational Focus, Structure, and Mindset as we naturally inherit societal paradigms in these three areas. To embrace a future-focused and effective organizational model, we will need to shift all three paradigms. To cause a paradigm shift is to cause a breakthrough. We need to see into the world of what *we don't know that we don't know*. Traditional learning is to take what we *know* we don't know (I *know that I do not know* how to fly an airplane) and learn the concept so that we now know it (I could take flying lessons and then claim I *do know* how to fly an airplane). But this book is about transformational learning – taking what *we don't know that we don't know* and making it known. Once you see the pragmatic simplicity in a new organizational model, you have choice - you can now choose to lead, manage, and work traditionally or effectively.

Here I combine multiple timeless proven practices into a simple unified system to create purposeful future-focused, effective, and efficient organizations. I have chosen a specific order to present concepts to ease your own transformation, as you and everyone else are accustomed to working in traditional ways and are currently at least partially blind to what is possible – you simply do not know what you do not know.

The simple and comprehensive organizational models presented here make it easy for anyone to embrace best practices – even those that are not experts in the alternative practices I propose. If you can understand and see information in a holistic view, you have a chance to see opportunities. This comprehensive model defines the design, operation, and performance management of an entire organization in a way for you to gain the benefit of much needed transformation.

Who benefits from reading this book?

Regardless of your role or industry, this book uncovers what you cannot see to create the desire for you to embrace a simpler way to create high performing organizations. Here is how to apply concepts presented in this book to improve your organizational performance.

Startups

You will learn how to design your organization right from the start to dramatically increase your chances of being successful. With what I propose, you can increase the power of your seed or investment capital, ensure strong employee alignment to deliver value and manage scalable growth with ease while creating a natural environment for innovation.

For-Profit Established Organizations

You will learn how to better focus and structure your company, and create an empowering cultural mindset, to simplify the management of your organization - creating unsurpassed results in all areas of organizational performance and a collaborative and joyful culture.

For Venture Capitalists:

Your judgment in selecting investment opportunities matters greatly. You cannot completely eliminate investment uncertainty in private equity, but you can dramatically reduce the risk by applying the recommendations in this book and simplify performing due diligence.

Nonprofits and Public Sector

You can ensure you are best serving your constituents through your organizations' heightened focus and ability. For charities, this means more people aided for the same donated dollar.

Healthcare, Educational, and Government Systems

You will gain the understanding that all organizations stem from the same foundational flaws, and we have an opportunity to take these currently broken systems and revitalize them into meaningful value-delivering institutions.

Change Agents

You will learn how the traditional environments you aim to improve either cannot embrace the change you propose or be successful in sustaining it. Knowing this allows you to recognize how these conventional environments will resist your recommendations and formulate a more effective approach.

I have aimed to make simple a complex subject; how to boost any organization's performance and create a collaborative and innovative culture quickly and completely. I am excited to have you realize what is truly possible – *achieving harmony and outstanding results need not be so hard.*

Together we can positively change economies, societies, and the environment. The basis of an economy is all about serving each other, and that is the first clue I offer you. *Simple* changes in organizational Focus, Structure, and Mindset can dramatically improve performance and cultural behavior not only for organizations, but for society.

What I propose in this book is not instinctive to traditionally trained people, which I believe is why the mainstream has yet to adopt a myriad of offered best practices that have been available to them for years. In this age of information, ignorance is no excuse. So why is a better way not adopted by the status quo? The concepts I propose are easy to learn and adopt, but *you must want to learn and adopt them. You must want to influence change, and I will bring a compelling argument for positive change.* I want you to see the sense and the simplicity in creating a powerful future of working together - cohesive organizations aimed at creating benefit for all concerned.

I invite you to be a part of furthering an abundant and productive future for us all. We can create greater cooperation than ever before.

The time is now.

TRADITIONAL PARADIGMS

PART ONE

"We take part in so many things that don't bring us joy, all in the name of "tradition."
- John Roedel

"To change an existing paradigm, you do not struggle to try to change the problematic model. You create a new model and make the old one obsolete."
– Buckminster Fuller

Are you a business owner that left the corporate world to create a business with a better work environment than you have experienced in the past? Here, I applaud you, and regret to say that as your company grows it will increasingly resemble the corporate world, simply because you will follow status quo business practices.

Are you a CEO who picked up this book thinking "What is it that I need to know?" so that you can create a Wildly Successful Enterprise? Or are you thinking that if you read this book, you can prove my recommendations to be incorrect?

Do you work in an organization, be it a business enterprise or healthcare, educational or government system, and you want to know what it is that you or your leadership does not know about creating healthy organizations?

Are you someone that consults to improve organizations, and like me, you are tired of the resistance you experience in bringing positive change?

Any way you come to read this book works.

Defining Terms

A common and incorrect assumption I have found in any business improvement endeavor is the assumption that everyone involved understands definitions of key terms. This is a false assumption. In working with two healthcare organizations, one a health insurer and one that provided disease management coaching to the insured population, I discovered that each had different definitions of key terms. Many of the key terms of the two organizations were common English words, and common terms in healthcare, so the team assumed that definitions were not necessary. After one month of joining the disease management company and gathering individual lists of customer issues from each leader, I noticed a common theme that people were using the term BENEFIT inconsistently. Being new to the company, I could get away with asking questions like "What do you mean by *benefits*?"

I came to realize that there were several disconnects in common term understanding and definition causing inaccurate data mapping to information systems, which had caused four years of program management challenges, difficulties for workers to use the systems without issue, and incorrect reporting. In fact, the customer was not happy with the company I worked for due to all the issues they experienced and that customer – the second largest customer to the company – was regretting that they had bought a new program the prior year.

Through a series of meetings over two weeks, I led teams from both organizations to define key terms, resulting in elimination of 50% of customer issues within three months simply due to miscommunication! As both sides corrected their process, system, and data errors related to these key terms, we began to gain traction to improve organizational performance.

I then led the next program implementation for our customer by applying best practices I propose in Part 2. That program was the first ever implemented without a myriad of problems. In fact, on go live day we had no problems at all. This renewed customer trust gave birth to new purchase agreements for an additional $40 Million of new disease management programs – all within my first year with the company.

The above example portrays how important assuring clear definitions can be, so I define key terms throughout the book to ensure agreement on their meaning with each definition as shown.

---

par·a·digm shift /perəˌdīm Shift/

Noun: a fundamental change in approach or underlying assumptions.

Definitions from Oxford Languages

Chapter 1

The Biggest Blindspot in Business

"Progress is a math formula. It only happens when the cost of the status quo is greater than the risk of change."

- Alan Webber

"I have always done it this way...is where dreams go to die."

– Mark Matson

By traditional organizational design, CEOs tend to be the most removed from the real problems faced in the business yet make decisions every day to improve its performance.

The potential payoffs for continuing to practice traditional methods for operating and leading an organization are:

- You get to be right or avoid being wrong
- Self-justification
- Magical thinking that you can follow conventional wisdom and get a different result
- Protecting your identity
- Minimizing problems with leading, managing or working in an organization
- Avoiding responsibility
- Fitting in

The cost of these payoffs is:

- Joy
- Fulfillment
- Peace of Mind
- Creating an organization where everyone can be Wildly Successful.

For those of you that no longer want to gamble your future investment of time and money into your business, organization, or career, you will learn a timeless proven method for designing, growing, and managing Wildly Successful Enterprises[SM].

The Iceberg of Ignorance

"When you change the way you look at things, the things you look at change."

- Wayne Dyer

The following study and illustration depict the degradation of information as you ascend the organizational hierarchy.

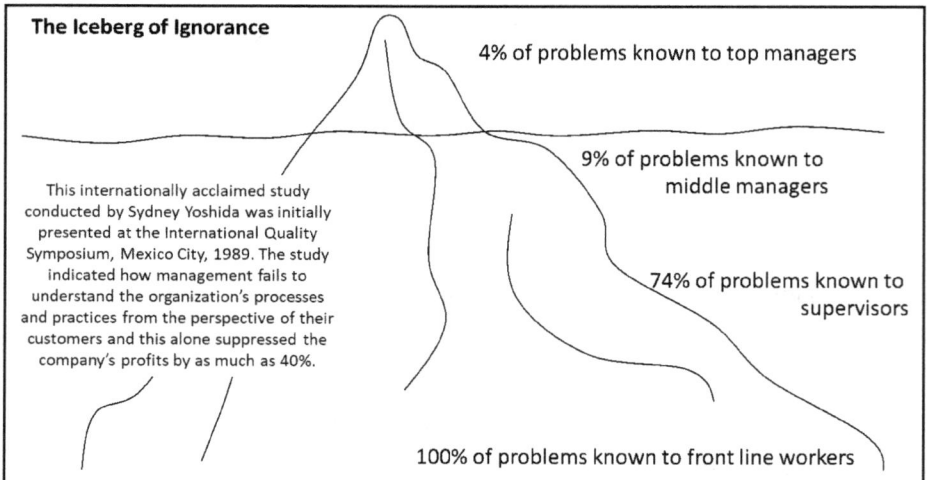

The Iceberg of Ignorance

4% of problems known to top managers

9% of problems known to middle managers

This internationally acclaimed study conducted by Sydney Yoshida was initially presented at the International Quality Symposium, Mexico City, 1989. The study indicated how management fails to understand the organization's processes and practices from the perspective of their customers and this alone suppressed the company's profits by as much as 40%.

74% of problems known to supervisors

100% of problems known to front line workers

Hierarchy Stifles Communication and Information Flow

Most people want to perform well and enjoy work. In the traditional paradigm, the genius of the workforce is highly untapped, with those at the bottom of the organization chart thought to be least important, *yet they are the majority - they know where many of the true problems lie.* Theoretically, the CEO should know the most about the company, but as the above illustration shows, this is not the case.

To what degree an organization is underperforming is related to its Focus, Structure, and Mindset, and as a traditionally run organization grows, the dysfunction grows exponentially. This ineffectiveness drives the need for more resources to address losses in efficiency and effectiveness, driving the price point for products and services higher and higher which puts pressure on the customer and eventually the economy.

Having analyzed the current state of many Fortune 100 companies I can confidently say that in each of them I uncovered hundreds of millions and even billions of dollars in opportunity in only a few short months. Additionally, critical services were taking months - instead of days or hours – for these organizations to deliver, affecting customers and in some cases costing lives. These issues were unrecognizable to leadership and most people in the organization. We tend to be oblivious to the water we swim in.

There are these two young fish swimming along and they happen to meet an older fish swimming the other way, who nods at them and says "Morning boys! How's the water?" The two young fish swim on for a bit, and then eventually one of them looks over at the other and says, "What the hell is water?"

"The point of the fish story is merely that the most obvious, important realities are often the ones that are hardest to see and talk about." - David Foster Wallace

---

The biggest blind spot in business is that traditional practices and organizational models do not allow for CEOs to see what is working well and not working well in their organizations.

Let us begin to remove the blind spots and see what we do not know that we do not know.

Chapter 2
Traditional Focus

"Always remember, your focus determines your reality."
                                                    — George Lucas

"Chase the vision, not the money; the money will end up following you."
                                                    - Tony Hsieh, CEO of Zappos

The primary focus of a CEO is to boost company equity, which traditionally is in their own best interest as that is where their incentives lie. In every organization I have been involved with, the main discussion in any townhall / all-hands meeting is about financial performance. The CFO will do most of the talking, sharing multiple financial terms and numbers.

The CEO and CFO will discuss their plan to improve these numbers. Most of this information is of little interest to the people working for them. Employees want to hear how leadership is going to make the organization work more effectively and be more enjoyable to work in. They want their work to be meaningful.

---

bal·ance sheet   /ˈbaləns ˌSHēt/

noun: a statement of the assets, liabilities, and capital of an organization at a particular point in time, detailing the balance of income and expenditure over the preceding period.

The balance sheet reports assets, liabilities, and equity, while the income statement reports revenue and expenses.

Scalefactor.com

With the primary focus of the CEO being that of creating equity, CEOs tend to have their primary focus involve financials. Unfortunately, financial measures **are latent *effects* of how the organization has performed, and do not directly show *what is working well, or not working well*,** in the organization.

Establishing a Balance Sheet, a traditional accounting method, forces the balancing of an organization's Assets against its Liabilities and Equity. I am going to explain some basic balance sheet principles to prove how focusing on the balance sheet drives the wrong behaviors in organizations.

A Simple Breakdown of the Balance Sheet

Equity = Assets – Liabilities

Traditional Key Assets: Cash, Accounts Receivable, Investments, Inventory

Traditional Key Liabilities: Accounts Payable, Taxes, Warranties

Flawed Traditional Accounting Assumption: *Inventory is an asset.*

Reality: *Inventory is a liability.*

The business has spared the expense to create inventory – or partially complete work –yet the business has not sold the work product, nor is there any guarantee that the inventory will sell, or the backlog of work needed.

In service organizations, inventories can be backlogs or queues of work, any delay of information to the customer. The longer the delay of producing a valuable service to the customer from this backlog of work, the less likely it is that this work will ever generate revenue.

This traditional accounting premise drives a wasteful behavior of allowing excess inventories when there are ways to ensure you can always meet your customer demands quickly without a buffer - large inventories or backlogs of work in queues.

With the traditional primary incentives set for CEOs to increase Equity, they tend to focus on increasing company Assets or decreasing company Liabilities. An asset that is under immediate control of the CEO is cash – usually sought after by increasing revenue. Another choice is to decrease operating expenses. As CEOs are mostly unaware of the detailed day-to-day operations of the company, they work to decrease expenses at the macro level by partnering with the CFO to improve the income equation by evaluating expenses from an accounting vantage point.

Point to Ponder:

Isn't it an interesting belief that the CFO can make financial outcomes of a company better, when revenue streams and the expense to produce products and services are a direct result of the day-to-day inner workings of the organization and not the result of the finance department?

An income statement is an equation of revenues, gains, expenses, and losses.

Income = (Revenues + Gains) – (Expenses + Losses)

With CEOs and CFOs focused on the macro level of the Income equation, the typical practices and behaviors that follow will increase income:
1. The CFO will work to control and cut the budget…
2. …which may require **downsizing** (reduction in personnel).

3. The CEO may engage in the search for a **Merger or Acquisition** opportunity – adding a company with good cash flow that can boost equity.
4. The CEO will set new **Arbitrary Goals** for leaders, thinking that meeting these new goals will move the financial numbers in a more positive direction.

These four practices – controlling and cutting the budget, downsizing, mergers and acquisitions, and setting arbitrary goals – are the first four practices we will discuss.

---

prac·tice /ˈpraktəs/

verb: Carry out or perform (a particular activity, method, or custom) habitually or regularly. "We still practice some of these activities today."

Similar: do, execute, apply, use, operate

Definitions from Oxford Languages

As you read on, reflect on your own professional experience, and see if you can identify with these practices and their impact on organizational performance, customer experience, and employee morale. *I specifically ask those of you who hold higher posts in organizations to envision yourself in the role of a front-line employee experiencing the effect of these practices.*

Traditional Practice #1: Budget Control

> *"Due to budget cuts, the light at the end of the tunnel has been turned off."*
> — *Aaron Paul*

In business, a customary practice is to create and manage a budget. Companies, depending on their size, will typically spend 3-18 months estimating what necessary expenditures will be for an upcoming annual budget. To ensure a safety net, as no one can predict the future, leaders will buffer their budgets. When finally implemented, budgets are overinflated, antiquated, and misrepresent actuality. Budgets can constrict organizations to adapt to what the future brings and often altered as the organization fails to meet goals we require even more effort applied toward manipulating a math problem. Instead of improving how an organization delivers value to assure satisfied customers and reliable cash flow, CEOs and CFOs cut budgets to improve how the organization looks financially for the short term, incapacitating the organization even more to produce value.

Who decided spending months creating budgets, only to reduce these budgets later, was a valuable effort? Who decided budget cutting was a smart thing to do? Traditional budgeting practices are just one of many traditional practices that waste time, money, and energy - all spent towards something that delivers far less value than the effort expended on creating it. Constricting how effectively an organization can function is like biting the hand that feeds you. We would all be better off focusing on delivering value to customers.

Are you directed regularly to cut X% from your departmental budget? Are critical changes needed to improve productivity, yet there is no room in the budget to make it happen? Do you have a solution that will solve a company-wide issue, yet the budget of another leader will need to contribute funds for the improvement and therefore, that leader has the power to deny progress? Does the business require new equipment or upgraded systems, but budget controls inhibit the investment in them?

Unable to Function

While observing the work performed by an onsite installation project manager, the biggest complaint I heard from her was that electronic diagrams for the installation were color coded, yet a recent budget cut included the removal of all color printers across the company. These project managers had to print the diagrams in black and white for installation personnel. The black and white diagrams left the installation to guess work, causing errors and rework at great expense. But the budget temporarily looked better. A financial leader had decided the cost of color printers was something they could eliminate easily without knowing the impact to the business and not accountable for the consequences.

If you went to a butcher shop to buy a steak and only had a $10 bill with you, and the steak you wanted cost $11, what would you do? Would you ask the butcher to cut off 10% of your steak?

No!

You would ask him to carefully trim the fat.

We badly butcher organizations by slashing expenses without recognizing the impact to the ability of the organization to function properly in its current state. Traditional accounting practices are hundreds of years old and focusing on them as primary measures will drive behavior that will degrade the business. Driving a business by the budget causes leaders to buffer their budgets in fear of losing necessary resources - creating an environment of scarcity with negative competition or collusion - while also inflating the budget! **Budgeting activity creates busy work, robbing the availability of vital resources that could contribute to delivering value to customers.**

More Budget Cuts

While listening to another request that year to cut budgets in a telecommunications engineering department, a VP and I had an instant messaging conversation:

Me: Hard to listen to - one of the biggest failings in business is the cutting of budgets across the board vs. finding where the waste really is, which when eliminated, streamlines the delivery flow to generate better revenue and faster cash flow cycles. I have already found where the waste really is.

VP: amen...leadership is spending so much unnecessarily on other things.

Me: but choke the delivery process instead

VP: yes

(Update on the VP: She understood the real problem, yet shortly thereafter removed from the organization due to questioning the sanity of actions proposed by executives. She was also the only woman of 4 VPs in this department)

The effect from budget cutting is often the dissemination of the delivery process, which is solely what generates revenue. Budget cutting is one of the key factors that cause tremendous and untraceable variation in financial and other performance measures, and in employee dissatisfaction.

Most leaders mistakenly assume the budget is the plan. Strategic planning will better help to prepare for the future than budgeting, yet every year leaders in traditionally operated organizations take part in a lengthy budgeting process to create a budget that will reduce productivity instead of spending that time on delivering more value to customers.

In summary, managing by budget drives the wrong behaviors:

- Streamlining efforts fail as leaders fear losing some of their budget the following year if they were to reduce operational costs.
- Leaders commonly pad their budgets for just-in-case scenarios.
- The organization loses agility to meet customer / market demands by needing to wait for the next budget to address them.
- Most budget processes take 3-18 months to complete, trying to predict the future (which is not possible) and tying up vital resources to produce a budget that is already out of date when implemented.

There are proven ways to create reliable cash flow which we will cover in Part 2. Progressive organizations that want to stand the test of time will practice them.

Traditional Practice #2: Downsizing

"As long as greed is stronger than compassion, there will always be suffering."

– Rusty Eric

"In the career world, we are downsizing. That means that the one person that will keep their job will do three or four jobs for the same amount of money. You have to be that way these days."

– Michelle Visage

We *do not* "have to be that way these days." It is the old paradigm that leaves no other choice in our minds. When needing to reduce expenses, often the first approach is to downsize the workforce, assumed to be the fastest and simplest short term expense reduction. Also assumed is that downsizing will create higher productivity, and the opposite is what occurs. What will happen is people will short-cut the process to try to keep up with demand, causing work needing correction further downstream, affecting productivity and the time it takes to deliver to the customer. Downsizing costs more than initial savings projections.

It was common back in my aerospace days for management to push for higher production to meet the monthly financial goals. I was able to prove that a higher percentage of customer returns occurred from parts produced during the end of the month rush.

A separate budget existed to address correcting the returns so that the production departments numbers look better.

Loss of knowledge of how to work certain processes occurs in every downsizing as traditionally run organizations are weak at capturing knowledge and process information. Tribal knowledge is prevalent in organizations and leaders have no idea how many pieces of an organization run based on someone's experience. It is normal to hear that employing people is the largest cost, but I would disagree— *losing knowledge and damaging the delivery flow causing loss of customers is far more costly.* Workers are in constant anticipation of the next layoff, as there is often little rationale for who stays and who goes. The impact on the performance and health and well-being of employees is overwhelmingly detrimental.

Dennis Muilenburg, the recently ousted CEO of Boeing, is leaving with a $62 million payout.

On the same day, 2800 workers lost their jobs because of the 737 Max issues, and unlike Muilenburg, they did not receive large exit packages but will receive 60 days' pay.

Adapted from https://www.businessinsider.com/boeing-muilenburg-payout-same-time-thousands-layoffs-2020-1

Interestingly, downsizing as a practice does not need to exist and is avoidable by simply ensuring the organization grows in a scalable fashion. Leaders need to recognize that **people are the organization's greatest assets instead of viewing employees as a liability on a balance sheet.**

When I engage with a new company, I perform Value Stream Analysis on the entire organization. The analysis uncovers so many systemic, process, and technology opportunities that it can be overwhelming. Most leaders are not aware of the value of this analysis.

One of the consistent issues I come across is the elimination of training development and delivery from a budget cut. This leaves workers receiving updated procedures, sometimes as often as weekly, without training, and expected to understand a constantly changing process and all content in every document to perform their jobs. This is idealistic thinking, for without end-to-end process engineering to assure a simple, yet powerful process and hands-on training followed by testing to ensure the worker understands the new or improved process, you are expecting miracles from your workforce.

As management continues to push for increased efficiency, quality suffers. Effectiveness (quality) is the predecessor to efficiency. If you take a little more time to do something right the first time you will be far better off then rushing through it and having to fix it later.

But first you must understand what to do to do your job well, and blindly cutting training personnel is a budget whacking approach with nothing but negative consequence.

When a downsizing occurs, employee confusion and frustration levels rise dramatically. The same result occurs with Mergers & Acquisitions.

Traditional Practice #3: Hidden Costs of Mergers and Acquisitions

"How do you make money? Spinoffs, split-ups, liquidations, mergers and acquisitions."

- Mario Gabelli

"80% of M&As fail to reach the goals and key performance indicators (KPIs) predicted."

- Graham Kenny (Harvard Business Review)

Mergers and acquisitions can expand market presence, allow a company to gain a new capability or product or service line, or take the good cash flow from one company and transfer that cash onto the financial books of the other. Mergers & Acquisitions (M&As) look better on the financial books than they ever prove to be.

According to Harvard Business Review, between 70% and 90% of mergers and acquisitions fail.

In my experience, mergers and acquisitions rarely allow for full maturity of the new larger organization, as the focus is on merging balance sheets to boost equity (which will only last for the short term). The vast expense and negative impact of a merger or acquisition is hard to measure, ignored, or cannot be well-addressed due to the traditional design of these merged organizations. Not fully addressed is the integration of cultures, work processes and information systems. A traditional merger or acquisition may improve cash flow in the short term, but over the long term will degrade product or service delivery processes and have departments fighting each other for survival while increasing expenses. The negative impact to customers is massive.

A former and trusted colleague that was working to improve a critical process with me sent an email one day after I questioned how she had missed something quite important to the process design. Sadly, her reply is all too common for people working in traditional organizations.

"I'm becoming a little numb to the disappointment because I've been with the organization for seven years now. When we first took over a large competitor shortly after I started, I had a challenging time.

*I tried to help with the integration of systems and processes, but after being beaten down for so long, I am willing to overlook the obvious. There are things you can change, and things you cannot. **The leadership in our organization is a cannot**."*

While working with a venture capital organization that had acquired and merged three businesses to create a new healthcare organization, a peer and I scoped twenty-one key integration projects necessary to ensure a viable future.

These projects, not predicted in the cost of the mergers, aimed to make the company whole. Six months after the merger, the CFO determined a budget cut necessary and laid us off.

All twenty-one projects lost momentum after that, and the company continued to struggle for years.

Traditional Practice #4: Arbitrary Goals and Bonuses

"There is an acceptance in the world of performing at less than excellence."

- Rose Hampton

Arbitrary goals based on balance sheet equations have detrimental consequences. "The goal this year is to improve speed to delivery by 20%!" Whether this is attainable or not is not in question, the goal has been set based on desired financial outcomes. This creates two scenarios:

1. Employees scoff at the arbitrary goal set by senior leadership, knowing that they cannot meet a goal without increasing expenses. They know that at the end of the year, Leaders will be able to make compelling excuses for not attaining these goals, and all forgiven.

2. Fearing their jobs, employees begin to work exorbitant hours with no increase in pay to try to hit the new goal. Some will look for new jobs (typically the more confident and capable talent) and leave the organization with a knowledge gap impeding the remaining team from supporting the effort. The workforce that remains can only attain mediocre performance, as they are the ones that will no longer challenge the status quo. All this strain and turmoil for an unrealistic goal – with the degradation of work-life balance to show for it.

Bonuses are set for executives to reach specific goals inside their departments that aim to improve the balance sheet equation. Whether these goals are the best incentives for leaders to pursue is already up for debate based on prior points made. The focus is all wrong. Manipulating numbers on the balance sheet does nothing to improve organizational performance. The impact on the workforce in trying to meet the latest set of arbitrary goals takes their focus away from delivering value and directs activity to what will artificially move the numbers.

A CEO, after reviewing monthly financial reports, sees that profit margins are declining and announces to their leadership team the need to increase the number of customer orders completed per month to generate more revenue sooner, which will improve the results for the next quarterly financial report.

Leader of Department A decides to increase production targets for his staff. The minimum acceptable number of orders has increased by 15%. His team jumps to work trying to meet the new goal, but there is now anxiety and fear amongst the crew. They know meeting or missing this goal decides their performance rating. If they complain that the new goal is unrealistic, they will not identify as team players, so they keep quiet and begin to work faster.

At the end of the month, Leader A is happy to see his goal met and proudly presents the new results to the CEO. "I am going to make my bonus" he proudly thinks to himself.

Unaware of changes in Department A, Leader of Department B is now becoming concerned as her team's ability to meet deadlines is decreasing. The work they are receiving now requires her team to correct orders, and since they know how to do this, they have taken on the extra work without complaint.

The following monthly financial report shows that customer orders are now taking longer to fulfill than last month. Reviewing the production numbers, it looks like Department B is at fault, as production is down 10% in that area and their backlog of orders is increasing.

The Leader of Department B claims she does not have enough people to meet demand and her requests denied for more staff, told to make it work with current resources!

Everyone in Department A is exhausted, and now that the pressure to perform is dissipating, they begin to return to former and more reasonable levels of work.

The ability for the organization to perform more effectively and efficiently has not improved and the workforce has become less engaged,

Setting arbitrary goals is damaging to both business performance and employee morale.

Ultimately, setting arbitrary bonuses and goals slows the revenue cycle and drives higher expense to deliver value to customers.

Focusing *solely* on growing equity creates the opposite effect. Efforts to improve financial outcomes, typically focused on three-month intervals to have the next quarterly financial report be more promising, drive a consistent **short-term focus**.

The author of The Soul of Money, Lynne Twist, states that Enron was an example of "get-mine-and-get-it-fast mentality – a mentality which only creates financial instability and proves to be unsustainable even if the short-term gains prove highly profitable."

Traditional accounting is based on a Chart of Accounts, a way to categorize the financial transactions that a company conducted during a specific accounting period. Accounts designate departments or functions, driving the need for creating divisions of labor, which influences the adoption of traditional organizational structure.

Chapter 3
Traditional Organizational Structure

"We cannot solve our problems with the same thinking we used to create them."

- Albert Einstein

We are all creatures of habit. Even the most spontaneous among us stick to routines and habits in life whether they serve us well or not. It can be challenging to try different approaches to how we work. When an entire organization is accustomed to doing things a certain way, even if it is not the best way, it is difficult to stop that momentum in a traditionally operated organization. Instead of trying to reverse that momentum by downsizing, budget cutting or reorganizing, **why not use that momentum and simply steer towards an easier path**?

If we want different results, we must try different approaches. The way we are naturally inclined to organize ourselves has us always create the same basic structure, and this common structure is NOT the best conduit to deliver products and services to your customers.

Your organizational structure decides how well your organization will perform (remember our teapot metaphor). The common structure that organizations take on is one of a top-down control, functional based hierarchy – primarily focused on managing people and controlling performance within segregated departments.

In reviewing definitions of hierarchy, it becomes clear how entrenched we are in living in them. It is ironic how our egotistical nature creates hierarchy which only results in stifling our ability to perform well. If your organization exists to supply valuable products and services to your customers, why not design it to do just that? Functionally based hierarchical design impedes an organization from reaching its maximum potential. Allow me to illustrate with a simple example of forming an organization.

---

hi·er·ar·chy ('hī(ə)ˌrärkē)

noun[1]

1. a system or organization in which people or groups are ranked one above the other according to status or authority.

"In the corporate hierarchy, Curt is about six levels below the CEO "

2. an arrangement or classification of things according to relative importance or inclusiveness.

*synonyms: order, **ranking, chain of command,** grading, ladder.*

Examples of hierarchy used in sentences[2]

"One of the first things you can learn by working at a large corporation is that everyone follows a strict hierarchy/chain-of-command."

"At most organizations, the CEO or President is at the top of the corporate hierarchy and maintenance staff is at the bottom."

"In this global society, there is a well-defined and alarming hierarchy that exists, separating the high born from the lower born."

1 Definitions from Oxford Languages   2http://www.businessdictionary.com/definition/hierarchy.html

---

Forming a Traditional Organization

In this example, we will use a simple product that someone has invented as example. Let us assume we have a powerful value proposition for our product – in other words, enough potential customers would find the product of value to them. Once the product proven to be valuable in the marketplace, the inventor of the product will want to make it available to the world, and so they will form a business to bring the product to market. Typically, this inventor will also take on the role of Chief Executive Officer (CEO) of the company.

The CEO will begin to attract various experts to direct the necessary functions for delivering this new product and for supporting the business. There is a need for a marketing expert to develop a brand and promote our new offering, thereby creating a demand for it. Another expert, a sales professional, to generate sales. To continuously improve the design of the product we require a research & development / product development lead, or the CEO may keep this responsibility for now. An operations expert will lead the manufacture, assembly, and delivery of the product. Lastly, a finance expert will account for cash flow, operational expenses, billing, payroll, and taxes.

The new business begins to form into the example structure depicted here:

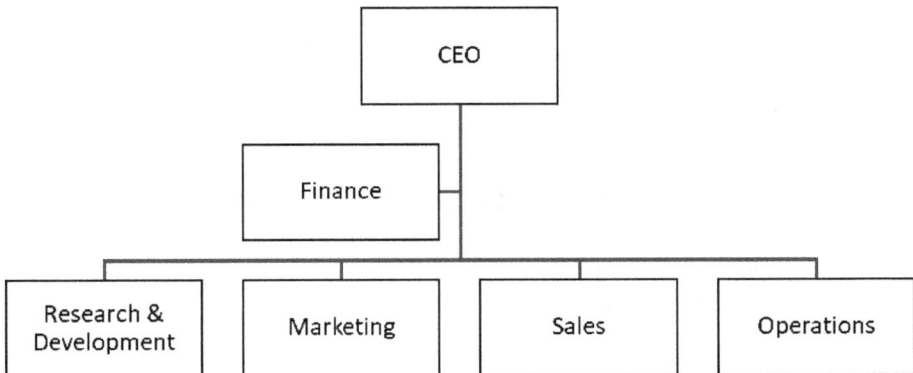

Startup Manufacturing Company Organizational Chart

In the beginning, this model can work. The organization is small enough that gaps in communication are rare, as there are formal lines of communication across all functions and involving all actors. There is little complexity with only a solitary product to concentrate on. There is an elevated level of collaboration as the team begins to assimilate into a traditional working model.

Assume we are successful at creating a demand for our product and the company is growing. We have added another product to our list of offerings. We now have a small manufacturing supply chain to manage, have expanded in-house engineering, and created assembly lines for both products.

As the business grows, our functional experts will become the heads of their departments as they begin to recruit others to help with all the tasks and responsibilities needed to support business demands in that specialty area. Our organization begins to look like this:

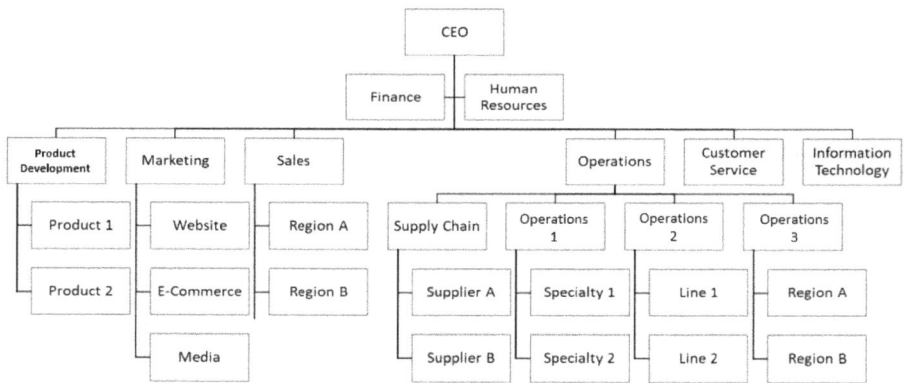

Small Manufacturing Company Organizational Chart

Let us assume our business continues to grow.

Research & Development has created two more product lines and each department is expanding and specializing to support these new products. More suppliers are necessary to fulfill on demand. We require additional engineering, assembly, and field service resources. Sales efforts are increasing, and the department is dividing again - now into four regions - to make it easier for the company to meet demand. Corporate customers have multiple locations do not fit into our regional model. Information Technology now has considerable infrastructure in place and is adding systems to help various departments perform their duties. The volume of calls from Customers requiring help with products, or requiring assistance with a problem, is large enough that we have formalized a customer service department. Our company now has a high enough number of employees to require a formal Human Resources department. The organizational chart for our business now looks like this:

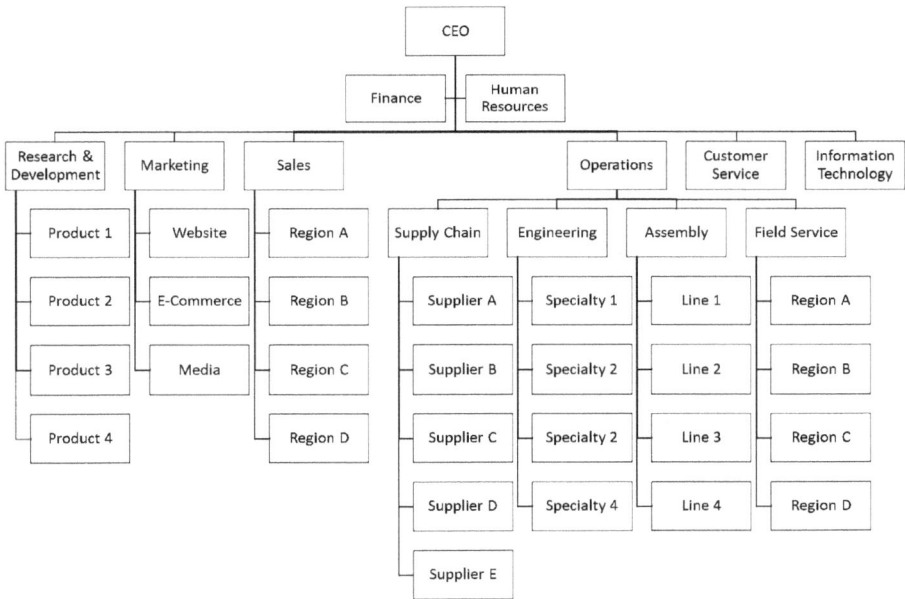

Mid-market Manufacturing Company Organizational Chart

Notice how this organization has grown organically as needs arise in the business. This business structure seems logical – this is a structure we are all used to.

Alas, collaboration is weakening with growth; it is only on occasion that one area asks another area what they are working on and about how to work with the rest of the organization. The good news is that Sales is selling like crazy and making big promises to customers. Uninformed of the big promises

Sales is making, the Operations department cannot buy equipment and hire fast enough to meet sales volumes to deliver to Customers. We are beginning to experience chaos in the organization as people try to mitigate issues, creating a higher volume of demands on Customer Service to deal with inquiries and complaints. Profit margins are falling, so the emphasis is for Sales to sell even more product, however they can, to increase revenues. We now require additional personnel to help with demand, track performance, and uncover issues in Operations to help meet targets.

Each department has target goals and is working to meet those measures. In turn, each leader begins to act on what they believe based on their experience is best for their department - the overall ability for the business to deliver is not the priority.

Contemplate the picture below. Superimposed on the organizational chart is a *simplified* view of a sole product delivery flow and the informal lines of communication in play across the business.

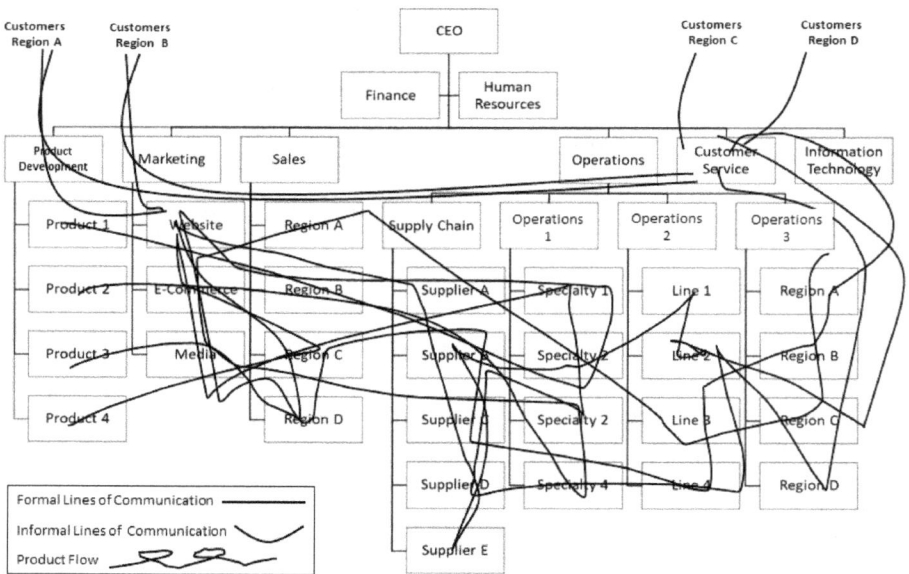

Organizational Chart depicting a single Product Delivery Flow and Informal Lines of Communication

As the business grows, this structure is creating increased complexity for the delivery of products and services. The lines of communication and the product or service delivery flow resembles spaghetti on a plate. Is this an efficient and effective way to run an organization? You may argue for a flatter organization – and the organization will still be functionally focused. Note: The lines shown are only a sole product delivery flow, and I have not included in-direct product or service workflows occurring in the organization, such as budgeting, hiring, and implementing technology.

What CEOs need to know is that the ineffectiveness of this structure negatively and directly affects customers and front-line employees while hindering the ability for top leadership to properly direct the organization. What is really happening in the organization does not directly affect or inform leadership. The above illustration portrays the sense of the dichotomy of work life experience between upper management and people working in the lower levels of the organization. There is far less complexity at the top; notice in the above illustration how the "spaghetti" does not touch upper management. That "spaghetti" is the livelihood of the business – if we cannot make our product well and on time, we lose customers.

As a senior leader, you may argue that you have "bigger fish to fry" than dealing with the minutia of day-to-day production and customer activities. **This is the first misunderstanding of the paradigm we live in; the "spaghetti" is where value generation is happening - *the organizational chart lines do not produce anything.***

I want to emphasize that the same reality – the "spaghetti" - exists in service and transactional organizations and is often vastly more intertwined. This is because service or transactional activities are intangible, making "products of work" more difficult and less obvious, and therefore the complexity of the workflow is not clear. I surmise that service and transactional operations struggle more with streamlining than manufacturing operations. Regardless of industry, operational flows are just one part of the whole organization. Today, manufacturing organizations are far more mature with their processes in the making of products than service organizations are at delivering services.

But regardless of industry, all organizations are lacking sound administrative processes in their organization. Every piece of an organization should focus on delivering value and assuring workflow is simple to follow and the process effective at delivering value.

Recall the balance sheet mentality. The typical reaction to losing customers is to find more of them. Most estimates suggest that it takes ten times more effort to gain new customers then to retain current customers. Why not focus on improving customer retention through effective value delivery? Notice that besides the organizational chart formal lines of communication, there are no other lines of communication to the senior leadership team. Direct communication from the customer occurs only with the sales team and field and customer service representatives. That customer feedback is also rarely if ever relayed to the people creating the products.

As a leader, I invite you to acknowledge the impact of continuing to promote this classic business model – organizing in a top-down functionally based hierarchical structure. From my experience, you have little idea of the scope of detrimental impact your decisions have on the people who are toiling to make the business work. And you are likely, quite frankly, to have a non-realistic understanding of *how* the people that make the business work are, in fact, really having to make the business work.

Not a highly effective way to run an organization, is it?

It is the paradigm most have chosen not to question.

The action of creating the same basic functional based hierarchical structure in organizations repeatedly is an automatic one, so we do not question it. As someone who has dissected how a myriad of organizations function at both broad and detailed levels, I usually have greater clarity than leaders about how the business is performing - as I am not a part of the hierarchy itself.

Hierarchical structures are so prevalent in society that we design software programs and systems for this premise. For instance, Microsoft® PowerPoint® software provides ten categories of SmartArt (see Insert menu) and one of those types is Hierarchy. Microsoft® Visio® (process flow chart software) has a complete set of shapes to generate organizational charts.

Google® has created Google Workspace® with Team collaboration tools can drive expanded engagement in several ways:

*A Google Docs collaboration **promotes transparency as employees in different departments** can see each other's drafts.*

*Google collaboration tools can create **new opportunities for communication, breaking down silos that damage efficiency**.*

*Employees have more **opportunities to share their expertise and build trust, rather than competing with one another**.*

https://www.wrike.com/blog/google-collaboration-tools-for-effective-teamwork/

Many major software companies have developed enterprise resource planning, communication, customer relationship management and workflow tools to better manage work across hierarchical boundaries. These systems help **lessen some damaging effects, but do not fundamentally solve the true cause of communication and delivery flow problems –** *the functional based hierarchy itself.*

The design of your organization drives behavior – design it carefully.

Why not design organizations to continuously flow work without interruption? Why not eliminate the cause of departments inefficiently competing with one another? Take your organizational chart and overlay it with another company's organizational chart. The same basic organizational structure will be clear. By changing the titles of five departments on our growing manufacturing business organizational chart, it now resembles that of a traditional health insurance company structure.

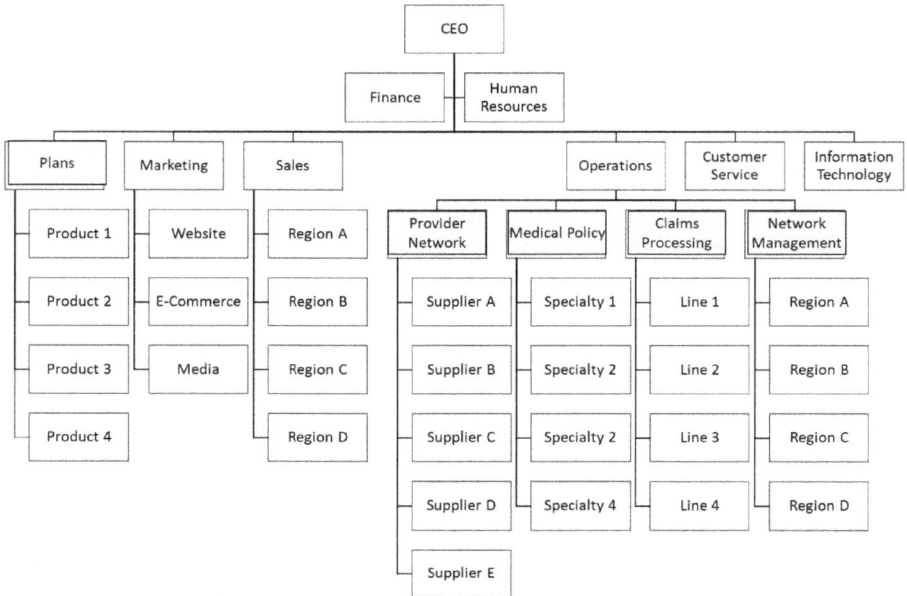

Manufacturing or Health Insurance Company?

My bet is that your organizational chart is fundamentally no different than that of other organizations and this common structure is a fundamental root cause of problems CEOs, employees, and customers face today.

Hierarchy is Detrimental for Human Cooperation – A Study

A study performed to test whether collaboration improved with hierarchy or without proved that **success and contribution decrease in hierarchically organized groups.**

"Achieving cooperation among humans is more difficult when there is an underlying hierarchical structure producing different ranks between people and therefore unequal payoffs for the participants."

Excerpt from https://www.nature.com/articles/srep18634

The very premise of traditional organizational structures is bankrupt. The way we humans have always organized ourselves is not best for delivering on a purpose. **Traditional business structure stifles collaboration, innovation, productivity, and profitability, and most importantly employee morale.** We need to take on a new structure – we need to swim in different water.

As a Traditional Organization Grows, So Does the Degree of Dysfunction

"So much of what we call management consists in making it difficult for people to work."
– Peter Drucker

Traditional organizational structures allow uncontrolled organic growth that absorbs profits and degrades collaboration. Like a gardener prunes a tree from the time it is a sapling to keep it strong and healthy, so must we care for our organizations. Allowing organizations to grow organically is analogous to a tree growing in the wild. A tree will grow more branches where there is propensity to grow in the short term, not necessarily in the best direction for them to grow in future years. A branch may become too heavy and split the tree trunk, other branches may grow downwards instead of up towards the light, others cross and tangle becoming malnourished. It becomes harder to tell if disease has set in due to the maze of branches.

Consider a tree structure analogous to an upside-down functionally based hierarchy, with larger branches being larger departments. A department leader will focus to keep their branch alive and even encourage growth, even if the branch is too heavy for the trunk of the tree. As the tree trunk begins to split (organizational dysfunction) we could invest in supports for the branch, tape the branch and trunk to keep the tree from splitting, or tie this branch to another affecting both branches ability to thrive. None of the aforementioned actions make the tree healthier. Focusing only on one branch is a myopic approach, analogous to leaders only focusing on their departments, as we ignore the impact to the entire organism. Yet, if we view the entire tree, it becomes clear that there is a better solution as depicted in the illustration below.

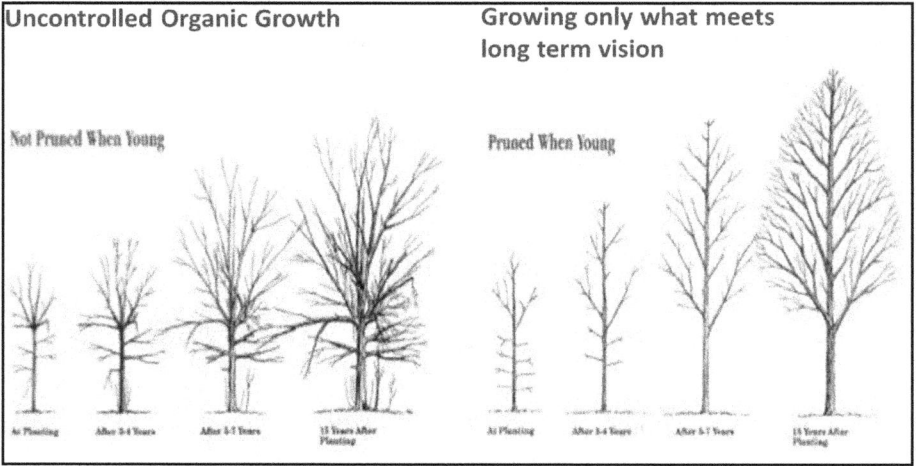

Organic vs Scaled Growth

Many of the leaders I have worked with did not try to get a whole and true view of their businesses. While the business continued to bear fruit, leaders continued to allow uncontrolled growth. Once the business began to fail, they stuck to traditional practices, and the result was disastrous.

---

*Eighteen months after my recruitment by a fast-growing mid-market healthcare analytics company, **I had developed a program implementation system that took the business unit I was serving from $50M to $90M in revenue.***

My vision was to replicate this system across the entire company, with the potential of increasing revenue - company-wide - by $200M or more. Unfortunately, I ran into resistance from Leadership, who were unwilling to leave conventional practices behind - even when I presented a proven new system!

As my business unit was winning new contracts, the company lost its largest customer and imploded overnight.

The company enforced a 20% budget cut across the board which included me and another colleague who was also not living near

Corporate Headquarters.

After the layoff, former customers I had interacted with contacted me via LinkedIn. They were in shock and genuinely concerned about the company's future abilities to manage the programs in which they had just invested. Every Director in the BU that I had supported began to look for other employment while the customer stopped investing in programs and allowed their contracts to run out. That new business unit folded within three years.

Back to the Budget

How does leadership typically turn an organization around financially when it is so handicapped? You start cutting branches—analogous to cutting budgets. When CFOs tell leaders to cut their budgets by a certain percentage, that is analogous to trimming every branch of a tree by that percentage. In an organically grown organization (represented by the tree on the left, below) does cutting all branches by an equal percentage create a healthier tree?

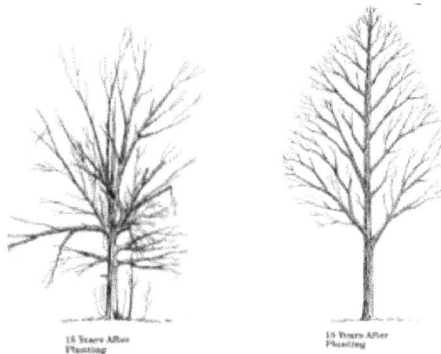

15 Years After Planting

15 Years After Planting

If the trees pictured above represent the structure of an organization, which one would you want to manage? Like a gardener's focus is on shaping a tree from the start to be strong and healthy, we can direct efficient growth of an organization, and in doing so we would never need to cut budgets after overspending, as the organization would only grow where necessary from the start. Part 2 of this book supplies an organizational model for you to design your business to run effectively indefinitely.

What is missing is analysis of what areas of the organization are unnecessary due to unchecked organic growth and which are healthy and should grow. Just like caring for a tree, we may need to cut entire branches to allow others to flourish. **Cutting across the board only looks good on paper and for the short term.**

Below are traditional practices that have arisen from top-down functionally based organizational structure.

Traditional Practice #5: Not Promoting all Types of Diversity

"We need diversity of thought in the world to face the new challenges."

– Tim Berners-Lee

The common organizational effort towards creating diversity relates to measuring the mix of cultural background or race. This focus has become a numbers game. One important consideration of diversity left untapped is the mixing of functional thinkers. To do that, besides hiring the right people for the job regardless of race, gender, age, physical handicaps, or economic background - all of which should be happening anyway - we need to avoid group think.

It is rare to find an organization that finds someone with another industry background an asset. My biggest challenge while working in healthcare was the lack of a clinical degree. What does a clinical degree teach you about how to design an organization for high performance?

---

group·think /gro͞op͵THiNGk/

noun NORTH AMERICAN the practice of thinking or making decisions as a group in a way that discourages creativity or individual responsibility.

Definitions from Oxford Languages

People that keep to the same industries soon begin to inherit long-standing assumptions and practices, not seeing opportunities outside of the world they have become accustomed to. They become unaware of the water they swim in.

The same concept applies to functional experts. We position functional experts in a particular area of an organization. Keeping people in functional groups detracts from diverse thinking, and therefore we lose tremendous opportunities to innovate or to solve problems. We hamper diversity of thought by keeping people constrained to their areas of knowledge. Cross-functional collaboration is difficult in a functionally based organization, yet the best results I have ever achieved is from engaging a cross-functional team.

The best leader I ever worked for was a black man from the Cooperative Republic of Guyana, eight years my senior in age. At the time he was the senior manager for supplier quality assurance in one of the largest aerospace prime supplier companies. In our 4,000-employee business unit, he was a cultural and racial minority.

He had a powerful vision. He formed his leadership team of three women and one man. He listened to our ideas and collaborated with us to bring tremendous positive change. A true leader, he defended and protected us from the naysayers (other leaders and even people in our own department) to do what was right. I consider him to be a very smart, brave, and ethical man.

The result was a total transformation of a 50-year-old supply chain to a leading-edge strategic sourcing accountability model, saving the company unmeasurable millions of dollars in administrative costs while improving suppliers' capabilities and quality of products.

By improving quality from 40% to 3% parts rejected by the turbine engine assembly line annually, we saved the company from even more expenditure. Every time an assembly line went down, Boeing would bill us $100,000 for every day's delay.

My passion lied in the fact that flight-critical components were of high quality.

I had graduated with my engineering degree only two years prior to working for him. The projects I led valiantly contributed to this initiatives' outstanding outcome – and I had no prior supply chain experience.

Traditional Practice #6: Positive Spin Communication

"A man can fail many times, but he isn't a failure until he begins to blame somebody else."

— *John Borroughs*

"The most important thing in communication is to hear what isn't being said."

- *Peter Drucker*

"Leaders who do not listen will eventually be surrounded by people who have nothing to say."

— *Andy Stanley*

I have recognized former colleagues having a natural inclination for pursuing excellence that often did not pursue opportunities for improvement. When I asked why, they said that they had their hand slapped too many times to bother trying ever again to contribute their talents to improve the organization.

Positive Spin

To put a positive spin on information means to communicate outcomes as better than actual, or simply leave out any negative fact.

Killing the messenger

To blame a problem on whoever reported it; to hold somebody accountable to a problem because he/she brought attention to it.

Here is a real-life excerpt of the experience of a dear friend of mine working in a traditional organization of 1400 employees. She read the first draft of this book, loved it, and replied:

"I could not understand why buyers were not competitively quoting

our supply base. Turns out people were miscoding commodity codes that tie the product to the supplier and causing issues for finance. So, our VP of Operations made the decision to drop commodity codes instead of fixing the coding problem! When I pushed and asked if the team who worked on this realized the chaotic impact to sourcing, informed that leadership had decided to "parking lot" it...TWO YEARS AGO!

Our buyers do not have to competitively quote now up to $150k! I was asked to shut up about the lack of commodity codes! Instead, I produced a stupid excel spreadsheet that allows the buyers to filter on supplier attributes. The buyers said it was the most useful thing they have seen in the company.

They have been restructuring our group with no direction for over 5 months (13 senior smart experienced people who could help restructuring) and our director is figuring it all out alone. Not one time asked to contribute.

I fear a major collapse is coming, but I will no longer be the canary that gets her head lopped off. Let it fail, just give me my paycheck.

I am bored and disengaged and I see it all over the place, in a company that touts its culture...culture is not volleyball and free snacks!

The CEO said in his all-hands meeting "you know how we feel about processes here" and everyone laughed. He said processes inhibit innovation... chaos ensues.... let us just keep hiring more people to cover it up. "

There is an undercurrent of dismay and complaint in organizations that goes unchecked. I have found listening to these complaints most valuable in solving major organizational issues – resulting in millions and billions of dollars in savings and revenue generation. Interestingly, over my career I have generated twenty times more revenue than I have ever reduced in operational expense, and I am not a marketing or sales professional.

I analyze the workings of an organization and present opportunities as fact – with data backing up every recommendation. Yet I have rarely experienced a management team that wanted to hear the naked truth about their business. *Why is that?*

The very nature of a hierarchy drives the behavior that a manager must know more than the people reporting to them. Couple that with the fact that as "experts" in the company, having someone else presenting opportunities they did not uncover themselves can drive a feeling of insecurity in people that are not confident, and they will discard evidence as unsubstantial. Passive aggressive cultures do not promote honesty, and the truth can be *unpleasant*. If you are not "nice" (meaning do not placate people) you do not fit the culture. Who wants to be a part of that kind of culture? I prefer being kind by being truthful. My career has involved getting leaders to understand a recommendation clearly enough to think the opportunity is their idea.

Most leaders are simply unaware of all the information one can gather about how an organization is performing. To make the best decisions, you need to know everything you can about an issue or subject. It is quite typical to experience people avoiding reporting negative consequences or outcomes, and this in turn drives leaders to make poor decisions due to lack of essential information. But poor leaders can hide in the hierarchy and look like they are performing well.

Traditional Practice #7: Measure Employee Performance

"Improvement efforts should focus on systems, processes, and methods, not on individual workers. Those efforts that focus on improving the attentiveness, carefulness, speed, etc., of individual workers — without changing the systems, processes, and methods — constitute a low-yield strategy with negligible short-term results. Conventional problem-solving would ask such questions as: Whose area is this? Who was supposed [to do this]? We don't ask "why," we ask "who." We don't look for causes in the system, we look for culprits in the work force. Performance appraisal is a "who-based" approach to problem-solving."

— W. Edwards Deming

Most employees have their performance measured to arbitrary goals set by leadership and have little to no control over what they can do to meet those goals. Pair this with the fact that one leader will subjectively review your performance only once a year and you can begin to feel the difficult position most employees find themselves in.

A survey of 7,500 full-time employees by Gallup found the top five reasons for burnout are:

- Unfair treatment at work

- Unmanageable workload

- Lack of role clarity

- Lack of communication and support from their manager

- Unreasonable time pressure

https://hbr.org/2019/12/burnout-is-about-your-workplace-not-your-people

---

Employee performance goals often do not reflect the constantly changing reality and lack rewarding employees for achieving milestones along the way. Behaviorally this drives cynicism and a "it doesn't matter what I do, it will never be enough" mentality. Additionally, since most goals are typically set as departmental goals, the overall chance of the company reaching its goals is low.

Only 23% of companies use a formal strategic planning process to make important strategic decisions.

https://www.thrivebusiness.ca/strategic-planning-key-success/

Most organizations do not develop strategic plans, and the fallout from lack of strategic planning is the inability to align people to meaningful goals. Therefore, performance reviews are subjective guesswork at best.

The number one practice in healthcare when a problem surfaced was to blame people, and the corrective action was to give them more training on a broken process.

Traditional Practice #8: Politics, Nepotism & Favoritism

"Politics is simply the organization of hatreds."

— Henry Adams

---

pol·i·tics   /ˈpäləˌtiks/

noun: activities within an organization that are aimed at improving someone's status or position and are typically considered to be devious or divisive.

"Yet another discussion of office politics and personalities"

nep·o·tism   /ˈnepəˌtizəm/

noun: the practice among those with power or influence of favoring relatives or friends, especially by giving them jobs.

"He promised an end to corruption and nepotism"

Similar: favoritism, preferential treatment

fa·vr·it·ism   /ˈfāv(ə)rəˌtizəm/

noun: the practice of giving unfair preferential treatment to one person or group at the expense of another.

Similar: partiality, partisanship

Definitions from Oxford Languages

A hierarchy is a structure that creates a particular mental attitude – those at the top considered more important than those at the bottom, becoming a breeding ground for politics. Politics and favoritism come into play in pursuit of money and/or recognition. When people, promoted past their capabilities are in charge they will manipulate situations to promote the illusion of business acumen and leadership. Hierarchies drive the behavior of having employees focus on making the boss look good vs. presenting fact. Since the design of traditional organizations influences the thinking that those at the top are more important those lower in the hierarchy, department heads work to control and manage people, creating a breeding ground for politics, favoritism, and nepotism.

I have often jokingly told people that I am too stupid to think of ways to undermine someone else, stating it would take far too much brainpower to invent scenarios to undermine others.

Politics, favoritism, and nepotism resemble the behaviors of a criminal internet data hacker – what a waste of brilliance spent on bringing others to their downfall.

A related topic is that of the empire builder, someone allowed to create and/or deliver a valuable capability for the organization while keeping any knowledge of how to produce this capability to themselves. This makes the empire builder the sole expert for a critical function and is due to lack of process focus and transparency. I have come across many empire builders in my career, working under the guise of helping the organization but secretly working to protect their livelihood. Empire builders thrive in traditional organizations.

Traditional Practice #9: Measuring What You Can

"Measurement is fabulous, unless you are measuring what's easy to measure as opposed to what's important"
                                                              – Seth Godin

Are most of your organizational metrics financially based? Are the key measures of the organization latent, reviewed long after the work that generated these results is complete? Do you measure what you can, not you should? Are technology systems misaligned, making it impossible to collect and discern meaningful information? Are workflows so chaotic that most data entered in systems is inaccurate? Is quality measured through sample auditing as systems cannot measure real-time results?

Most organizations organically grow with little thought about what and how to measure that which will keep the business strong and healthy. We measure macro level latent financial results instead of how well we are performing in the delivery of products and services. We do not measure how capable we are as an organization to deliver customer value. I am amazed at the number of technology systems I have encountered that do not capture fundamental data that would help the business improve.

I can say most measurements in organizations are finance or compliance related and considered most necessary due to the wrong focus, resulting in leaders being ill-informed of what is really happening in the organization and making poor decisions because of it.

Decisions like…

Traditional Practice #10: Reorganization

> *"We trained hard, but it seemed that every time we were beginning to form up into teams, we would be reorganized. I was to learn later in life that we tend to meet any new situation by reorganizing; and a wonderful method it can be for creating the illusion of progress while producing confusion, inefficiency, and demoralization."*
> *– Gaius Petronius Arbiter (c. 27-66AD)*

Gaius Petronius Arbiter, a Roman courtier during the reign of Nero, believed to be the author of the Satyricon, a satirical novel written during the Neronian era (54-68 AD) [adapted from Wikipedia]. Even two thousand years ago, Arbiter could realize the folly in organizational practices that continue to this day. Reorganization is a practice that has existed over millennia.

Reorganization (also referred to as a "re-org") is an infamous attempt to achieve better business results through rearranging the experts and people into another hierarchical structure. The typical cadence for reorganization occurs every 4-12 months, often triggered by results reported after the closing of the fiscal quarterly or yearly report. Executives "shuffle the personnel deck" in a feeble attempt to improve performance. Imagine being a card in that shuffle repeatedly. For many of you reading this, you do not need to imagine it, the experience is all too real.

Sixty-nine percent of companies restructured their teams during the Covid-19 pandemic.[1]

1 The Predictive Index | Annual CEO Benchmarking Report 2021

Reorganizations change how people in the business report to certain leaders. Some leaders may inherit new titles, some departments renamed. The attempt by the CEO and the senior leadership team is to shuffle leader responsibilities in the guise of delivering better results as a way to better align people to gain efficiency. As a CEOs traditional focus is to boost equity, reorganizations are temporary attempts to achieve this. Re-orgs are especially predictable when a new leader joins the company, thinking that their new business design will be an improvement on that of past leaders.

Re-orgs are often an attempt to drive improvement through new alignment, but typically have an opposite effect as people working in the organization become more confused with each change as to how their work connects to processes in other parts of the organization. With reorganization comes growing confusion about alignment to goals. In modern times, with the advent of the industrial revolution and technology, our natural inclination to organize and re-organize top-down functionally based hierarchies has created further detrimental effects on organizational cultures.

In large companies, like the Fortune 1000, reorganizations have become ridiculously frequent and are costly and pointless attempts to rearrange people in a more efficient and effective way. The same basic structure still exists in the end; people reporting to people in departments.

Common reactions to reorganizations from tenured employees are:

"That project derailed after the last re-org."

"They keep reorganizing us, we can never get any traction."

"This is my fourth manager change this year – I have no idea what I am supposed to be working on."

"The latest organizational structure is the same as it was 10 years ago, and it didn't work then!"

The cost of moving people can be high; the loss in productivity is unmeasurable. A reorganization will allow most or all issues affecting performance to continue to flourish. The employee experience is that of a work environment so disorganized that their day consists of trying to get back on track. Ironically, the reorganization will result in a top-down functionally based hierarchical structure that will generate the same intrinsic issues. Workers in the organization live in fear and resignation because budget-cutting, reorganization and downsizing typically occur in perpetual cycles, with the fallout being the need to continuously and quickly fix problems generated from such actions. Quick fixing becomes a cultural mindset.

Chapter 4

Traditional Mindset

"Action expresses priorities."

— Mahatma Gandhi

A focus on short term financial gain combined with functionally based hierarchical structure creates dysfunctional behaviors at all levels, perpetuating the same basic problems in any organization. Focusing on improving financial performance weaken business performance as financial information is insufficient for solving organizational issues. Functionally based hierarchical structures compound the inability to solve organizational issues by dismembering communication and delivery flow.

In this chapter I will share how issues generated from the wrong focus and structure tend to be reacted to with weak problem-solving approaches. We have become a society impatient to get results, and so it is understandable why many leaders and their organizations have developed a mindset to quick fix problems. The prevalent focus in business (and government politics) is short term gain and is the fundamental reason for budget cuts, reductions-in-force (government shutdowns), and reorganizations (new administrations) being commonplace.

Let us review problem-solving practices that are in play in traditionally focused and structured organizations.

Traditional Mindset #11: Rewarding Quick Fixes

"One of the true tests of leadership is the ability to recognize a problem before it becomes an emergency."

- Arnold Glasow

Many CEOs struggle with managing growth since the organization is in no way set up to handle growth. Without good structure, an attempt to grow an organization will either take excessive resources or fail altogether. To give a sense of impact, I have found billions in waste in Fortune 100 companies in only a few months of analysis, opportunities hidden from leaderships view. Most leaders cannot see the waste in an organization as they are not aware of how to find it.

Compounding the issues created from the wrong focus and structure is the encouraging of quick fixes in the form of workarounds.

The Workaround

"Most people spend more time and energy going around problems than in trying to solve them."

– Henry Ford

Workarounds create extra burden by requiring special oversight and management, as they veer from the normal delivery processes.

Workaround

A temporary process (quick fix) put in place to alleviate the effect of a problem.

Workarounds hide the effect of the issue they are to temporarily address because they tend to become permanent processes entrenched into daily routine as the effect of the issue dissipates. Workarounds often surface with changes in products and services, with growth, and after a recent technology implementation. Due to inadequate process analysis and streamlining prior to development, most technology cannot adequately support value delivery flow and organizational capabilities. Combine this with typical project overruns or budget cuts that stop full development or proper implementations of the technology and you have just created more inefficiency and ineffectiveness at great cost.

Multitudes of businesses, healthcare, education and government systems waste billions of dollars and delay services to customers due to workarounds. Another term for workarounds is band-aid solutioning, a term derived from the popular BAND-AID® brand of adhesive bandages that help to protect small wounds. There is an excessive cost associated with not solving problems wholly and completely. It is common to experience a lack of patience by leadership to do the right thing. This lack of patience exists due to short term financial focus and needing to look good come financial reporting time.

The quick fix mindset coupled with unbridled organic growth creates extremely unstable organizations. Due to rewarding people that put quick fixes in place when problems strike, these organizations run with excessive heavy lifting by employees to make the organization work. These quick fixes, or "band-aids," create layers of unsustainability as one urgent issue after another is covered-up as quickly as possible. Workarounds never solve the true problem and only dampen the effect.

Once the negative effect of a problem dissipates, rarely does leadership look back to measure the long-term effect of the temporary fix, nor try to create a long-term sustainable solution, as leaders no longer experience the pain. Leadership is not concerned with the long-term effects of a quick fix, as they will either move on by promotion, by leaving the organization, or due to the next reorganization. The quick-fix approach to problem solving (actually nothing but problem cover up) has employees running "helter-skelter" to appease leadership and drives a trial-and-error mentality. Directing employees to quickly resolve (band-aid) an issue is a huge mistake, as all that the quick fix will accomplish is to cause more chaos in the system. Common phrases in the workplace are:

"We throw it on the wall and see if it sticks."

"In this organization, we perform dartboard solutioning."

"Leadership only wants to hear that the solution works, whether it does or not."

"Fire, Ready, Aim"

"All we do is firefighting here."

The prevalent focus in business is short term gain and is the fundamental reason budget cuts, reductions-in-force, and reorganizations are commonplace today. Most members of organizational leadership are in their roles solely because they continue to "save the day" with little accountability for the unsustainable situation created. Many businesses are precariously functioning due to this behavior and some employees know it. Others know no other way to react to problems, especially if they have been with the company for a long time. "Just put the fire out" is normal leadership guidance – and it becomes the cultural mindset. **The impact of the quick fixing mindset is that there is rarely interest in understanding why the problem surfaced in the first place, nor on the number of resources quick fixing consumes in delivering unsustainable and unreliable solutions.**

A "get it done now" mentality drives poor decision-making. We may stop the bleeding, but leaders are not accountable for long-term fallout due to weak solutions: decisions made without seeking all necessary information. Rarely are leaders held to long-term goal incentives that could drive a different behavior.

Case Study: The Cost of Quick Fixing: No longer the Industry Leader

"Any manager can do well in an expanding market."
– W. Edwards Deming

Scenario: A forerunner in online education losing 10% market share annually for the past four years.

I could feel the dysfunctional heaviness after only two weeks of coming onboard. Sensing the disconnects, I named the core processes of the organization, and performed an assessment of all three of these critical processes across the organization.

While performing process analysis, I would ask where to go to continue to follow the process. People would say something like "I think that is in Sue's area." When I would ask what "Sue's area" was responsible for, most did not know, only that "Sue" was in charge. Functionally focused segregated departments and sub-departments prevailed.

Within six months, I had found $125 million in wasted effort resulting from chronic quick fixing including band-aided processes and piecemeal technologies. The $125M was what I could easily calculate, the positive ripple effects immeasurable.

I presented my analysis to the Chief Operations Officer (COO), and he did not take the news very well. $125M of waste found inside his organization. He spoke about how devoted he was to the company that had professionally raised him from the age of eighteen, yet at 36 years of age he was unwilling to do what it would take to save it.

In fact, the COO did not even publicly acknowledge the analysis. He was unwilling to transform an overgrown and weakly controlled organization into a Wildly Successful Enterprise.

Instead, he laid off our entire team of business process engineers and project managers with the belief that tenured people in the organization could replicate our ability.

The following year the COO was fired after an evaluation of the leadership team.

Traditional Practice #12: Brainstorming

"One accurate measurement is worth a thousand expert opinions."
– Grace Hopper

Brainstorming has become the modern term for calling a meeting.

Actual Brainstorming is a solution generation method that, when applied correctly, can help to drive innovative opportunities.

When presented with a problem or goal, is the next action to pull a group of managers or directors together to brainstorm a solution? After most meetings, do you find nothing resolved and another meeting scheduled? Are there individuals who do all the talking while others sit and listen, never asked for input? Are decisions made based on opinion or based on data?

A weakened form of brainstorming is prevalent in today's organizations. Brainstorming has become the common term for problem solving and is usually an *uncontrolled discussion of what might fix an undefined problem, usually involving the wrong actors.* Often, the recommendation from the loudest or highest in power will prevail and their untested solution implemented. Another uncontrolled change in process, or a reorganization, will unravel the solution and another problem will rear its ugly head. I describe the method of Brainstorming in Part 2.

Traditional Practice #13: Implementing New Technology to Fix Problems

"The key to digital transformation is re-envisioning and driving change in HOW the company operates. That's a management and people challenge, not a technology one." **- Digital Transformation Report © 2011 MIT Center for Digital Business / Capgemini Consulting**

"At least 40% of all businesses will die in the next ten years… if they don't figure out how to change their entire company to accommodate new technologies."
– John Chambers, Executive Chairman, CISCO Systems

The current trend is to solve business problems with new technology systems and automation. Typically, there is a business vs. information technology mindset in organizations due to hierarchical structure. Even with this internal conflict, technology is more often the choice to solve business problems that technology cannot solve, such as lack of value delivery focus or hierarchical organizational structure.

Due to the traditional organizational structure, the technology department has no hope of being successful in solving the businesses problems. The understaffed Information Technology (IT) department foregoes taking time for documenting processes and technology, so that future support of technology and the business becomes an issue.

All of us have contacted a technical customer service group in some form or fashion to get help with software or hardware issues - this is a demand management process.

This type of process takes information from the customer about the issue and triages the problem to route the customer to the proper technical help. The same goes for software development, who take input from people in the organization who are working with an application (technology system) that is not working as intended. This can be due to a failure in the technology infrastructure (hardware) or in the software design.

I have redesigned demand management processes for many technical departments, and I have never found the process well designed or measured.

Typically, these processes follow the same basic construct:

INTAKE ➔ *TRIAGE* ➔ *PROBLEM-SOLVING* ➔ *CORRECTION or NEW DEVELOPMENT*

Recently, I worked to correct a demand management process that was absorbing precious resources in trying to understand what the problem was.

All the Requestor needed to send a request was a brief description and the name of the application. Since humans like to solve things, usually the Requestor would supply a solution to whatever they were experiencing. There was no accountability for the submitter to define the actual problem.

After a series of steps, to include a prioritization process that only occurred monthly (subjectively biased with weak information), a developer would receive the request. With the trail cold, now the developer (expensive resource) would schedule meeting upon meeting to get the root of what the real problem was and what the process was that Requestor was working to improve that caused them to ask for their solution.

Based on this limited information, development work would begin without any business justification. The number of tickets closed was the only measurement of this process.

Measuring how long the entire process or phases of the process took did not occur. No measure of the number of hours spent on development per request. There was no measure of quality of work or outcomes. No accountability to prove that the effort was a gain for the organization.

I am never surprised, but always shocked, to imagine how Fortune 100 companies are even functioning, as I have yet to find one with a healthy, well-measured process. And small companies do the same things, but harboring inefficiency is not a small business luxury.

Technology systems do not create better efficiency or effectiveness in delivering value to customers when the processes they automate are ineffective to begin with.

The IT profession has developed many best practices and models the whole organization can use, but rarely adapt. In traditional organizations, Organizational and Business Architecture are ill-designed and /or ill-defined, leading to many leaders leaning on technology to improve organizational performance and creating difficulty in technology implementations. Here I primarily concentrate on improving Organizational and Business Architecture as without these being well designed, all other effort is based on weak structures. Although the IT profession has devised six architecture types for business, the profession itself does not address organizational architecture and defines business architecture related to technology instead of processes.

Organizations spend billions of dollars annually engaging large consultant firms to prepare them for significant technology lifts. These firms tend to interview people across the business, collecting knowledge already known to workers and not to management, and then generate beautiful presentations depicting findings and plans that sound impressive yet are highly unactionable. Here, the organization has not gained the ability to re-design or improve its organizational or business architecture, and typically these consultancy firms leave no useable documentation when they leave. Without improvements in organizational and business architectures, the multi-million-dollar technology implemented with many old practices, processes and workarounds hard-coded into the system is the result. Certainly not a desirable outcome.

I will share an adaptable, value focused organizational architecture, proven practices for well-defined business architecture and technology development in Part 2.

Traditional Practice #14: Perpetual Projects & Assuming Infinite Resources

"Failing to plan is planning to fail"

– Benjamin Franklin

Are you working after hours just to get your "day job" completed? Do you need to cancel personal plans to meet deadlines? Is your schedule full of overlapping meetings? Are you currently assigned too many projects to keep up with? Do projects tend to last for what seems like eternity – or never completed? Do necessary projects never get off the ground? Are there never enough resources available to get everything done? Are projects chosen through brainstorming annually during budget season? Are there "pet" projects in play, meaning someone's "great" yet unproven idea that serves their agenda? Did you ever find out about a project that is well underway in another part of the organization that is changing your workflow without input from your department? Did you ever find out about a duplicate project in another area of the organization? Do leaders in your organization start up projects without consulting with other leaders?

A dear friend and fellow Author recounts:

As we were developing a new product, we discovered another department was working on the exact same thing. Both departments were working in a vacuum. All those resources wasted versus collaborating on the solution. Here we were competing to produce the same outcome. Leadership never addressed this competition; they decided to allow all of it to continue. I left the organization after that.

One of the biggest failings I find in organizations is the ability to prioritize work, consuming excess resources for too long on far too many efforts that are not worth working on in the first place, akin to novice gardeners taping or propping up branches without tending to the tree.

It is usually the IT department that leads the organization in creating project governance processes through the development of a Project Management Office (PMO) that ensures project management professionals are managing technology projects. Just because someone has managed projects, it does not make them a Project Manager. IT will practice project management to better manage all the many projects that include technology lifts to best use a finite group of human resources. Typically, other business leaders can launch projects as they see fit - without a strong business case and tie up resources that should be working on more important projects. Business leaders can launch projects without governance and justification.

Governance refers to structures and processes designed to ensure accountability, transparency, responsiveness, rule of law, stability, equity and inclusiveness, empowerment, and broad-based participation.

Adapted from http://www.ibe.unesco.org/

Lack of governance leads to lack of the prioritization of what the organization should be working on. Consider the possibility that there are ways to get more accomplished in less time with fewer resources - because there are.

A Note on Organizational Culture

"Traditional organizational culture is based on placating the leaders above you, and that behavior is driven by functionally-based hierarchy being the dominant structure of organizations."
– Dawn Holly Johnson

Organizational Cultural Attributes

*Organizational culture is based on shared **attitudes**, **beliefs**, **customs**, and written and unwritten **rules** developed over time and **considered valid**.*

---

*Culture **decides** how **power** and **information flow** through its **hierarchy**, and **how committed employees are towards collective goals**.*

*Culture **affects** the organization's **productivity** and **performance** and is unique for every organization and **one of the hardest things to change**.*

Adapted from businessdictionary.com

Organizational Culture does NOT need to be "*one of the hardest things to change*." The wrong organizational Focus, Structure, and Mindset make change difficult.

We might as well believe the earth is flat.

Chapter 5

Working in a 2-Dimensional World

"If you stay in this world, you will never learn another one."
— W. Edwards Deming

"The church says the earth is flat, but I know that it is round, for I have seen the shadow on the moon, and I have more faith in a shadow than in the church."
— Ferdinand Magellan

The Greek philosopher Aristotle (384-322 BC) argued that the Earth was round, due to the circular shadow it cast upon the Moon during a lunar eclipse and as some stars are visible from Egypt but not visible at northern latitudes.

Most of the civilized world believed the earth was round by 800AD, including Christian philosophers and Muslim Arabs who recognized these claims.

Adapted from http://launchistory.blogspot.com/2012/06/history-of-round-earth-theory.html

---

To this day, some people still believe that Christopher Columbus 'sailed the ocean blue in 1492' to prove the earth was round. He was, in fact, hoping to prove that it was faster to travel to India by sailing west then by sailing east from Spain. At the time, correct calculations of the distance around the earth existed, as did agreement that the earth was in fact round. Because of this, King

Ferdinand of Spain knew that traveling west was a much longer route than traveling east and denied Columbus funding. Columbus convinced Queen Isabella to fund him after adjusting calculations to proclaim the distance west from Spain to India was one fourth of the then current accepted standard.

In the United States, Columbus Day is a national holiday recognizing his arrival in America. It is common knowledge that the Vikings landed in North America several centuries earlier than Columbus. Current theory is that the first humans to discover the Americas migrated over the land bridge from Asia over 15,000 years ago.

I make these points to demonstrate that *we love tradition more than fact.* Many of the best practices I will present in Part 2 of this book have existed for decades yet remain ignored by the mainstream. Why do we hold onto traditions that drive injurious behavior and poor performance? Because we gravitate to the status quo, no matter how painful the experience. Just as when people believed the earth was flat, we continue today to work in a flat, two-dimensional world.

Traditional 2-Dimensional Thinking

Natural human tendencies have us work to improve only two dimensions in business - People and Technology:

1 People

Traditionally, the dimension we focus on primarily is People. We look up to and follow the people in charge, listen to experts, and manage staff. We align people to managers instead of to the work necessary to deliver on our organizational value proposition. We do need to align people, but it is what we align them to that makes all the difference. We really do not need to micromanage people when we are all working on the same focus and in the right construct. If you listen to the people that work in the direct delivery of your products and services you will learn much about improving your organizational performance, yet rarely do I see this advantage taken. Traditional focus is on managing people, not delivering value.

2 Technology

> *"It is often said that 'data is the new oil.' Instead, we'd argue that it's trust that will decide whether businesses – and the Fourth Industrial Revolution itself – succeed. There is both a moral and business imperative to do more than increase profits. My fellow CFOs and other leaders should respond to today's rapid technological and societal change by taking a long-term view."*
> *- Mark Hawkins, President and Chief Financial Officer, Salesforce*

The other dimension that is traditionally focused on is Technology. Society began to place emphasis on technology as the industrial revolution evolved with mechanical innovations. Once computing technology began to surface, the service revolution was born. As the service revolution surged, the answer to every operational problem was to implement an information management or workflow system. Now we are in the era of digital transformation.

Information and workflow systems such as Enterprise Requirements Planning (ERP), Customer Relationship Management (CRM), accounting systems and the like considered the leading technologies that will tie an organization together. Technology cannot solve the root cause of issues in a top-down functionally based hierarchical structure, as we traditionally apply technology on top of segregated groups and messy processes. The fourth industrial revolution is digital transformation, in which companies are simply using bots and other "quick" automation tools to automate poorly defined business architecture. Data structures are therefore hierarchically driven, instead of value delivery driven.

A Note to Software Companies

Although tech companies create software to alleviate some of the challenges a traditionally design organization experiences, often the design of technology occurs without first engineering processes to be effective. Rarely is software evaluated by objective people – folks that did not participate in the design of the technology, so problems with user experience go unnoticed. Technology becomes more difficult and expensive to change over time. There is a way to circumvent this problem that I will discuss in a future chapter. Also, rarely does a software company supply process flows to show how everything will work. Instead, we train people that will use the technology on how to use various screens applicable to their role – as they stay unaware of the entire process and benefits of the system. This is a dangerous practice, as now people with limited purview will make poor decisions due to lack of awareness of the design of the end-to-end process and technology solution.

I have come to recognize five flawed assumptions within the traditional organizational paradigm that perpetuate this 2-dimensional thinking.

The 5 Flawed Assumptions

1. *People (everyone in the organization) know and understand what their customers value.*
2. *People (everyone in the organization) know what part they play in delivering value.*
3. *People (functional experts) are great leaders and managers.*
4. *People (functional experts) are great business designers.*
5. *Technology will* always improve how People work.

Let us address each of these assumptions in greater depth.

Assumption #1: People know and understand what their customers value.

We covered the importance of everyone in your organization knowing and understanding your value proposition. Do not continue to assume you know what your potential customers want and need. What we each value is highly personal, and we cannot assume we know what someone else values.

When I joined a 49-year-old Fortune 1000 company I discovered that they had just begun their first true customer experience inquiry— directly listening to customers for the first time with tenured employees shocked to hear what the customer really wanted.

These tenured employees admitted to having assumed they themselves knew what customers wanted when developing and redesigning product and service delivery mechanisms over the years. They also admitted to sometimes creating the exact opposite outcome from what they had recently discovered their customers valued.

I saw that although they were now finally asking for Customer input, they had already designed a customer service online portal and then began asking leading questions in gathering feedback.

They ignored asking the customer what was missing in interacting with the organization in the first place and basing the design of that portal on Customer needs.

A kind soul who reviewed the draft manuscript of this book, offered her own experience:

As a young CPA, I moved after two years from one international accounting firm to another. The two firms had vastly different approaches and policies.

Shortly after joining the second firm, during a staff meeting intended to generate new clients, I asked what differentiated our firm from any of the other "Big 8".

"Why would clients want to come to our firm?" I asked.

The greeting I received was veiled scorn by partners and managers of a rigidly antiquated profession who's only answer was "Because we are XYZ Accounting, everyone knows we are great."

They completely missed the point of the question and their arrogance caused them to ignore a huge opportunity of discovering what their clients valued.

Any particular definition of value is a temporary phenomenon, subject to change based on innumerable factors. The inability to adapt and innovate can affect an organization's value offering. A highly popular offering can become obsolete. Do you recall the entrance of the new Apple iPod and the introduction to .mp3 (audio) files into the music industry? Goodbye CDs! Notice that those that adapted quickly to this new and intangible product succeeded in the music industry.

Assumption #2: People know what part they play in delivering value.

We are at our best when we work together, and cooperation is crucial to generate maximum value. Working within the confines of a top-down functionally based organizational hierarchy does not allow for cooperation to occur naturally. When we align our business structure to delivering value, the processes become transparent – **designed so that people working those processes inherently know when they provide value to customers, and when they do not.**

It is commonplace today to play it safe when presenting new innovative ways to work that may challenge leadership. In a traditional organization, the senior leadership team begins to take on group think, as rarely do they engage with the people in the lower echelon performing the work that directly delivers value. Every person thinks differently about challenges or opportunities, which contributes to diverse thinking. Underutilizing the work force impedes the generation of value by stifling creativity. The traditional focus on business functions degrades the ability for participants to see how they contribute to the whole.

Assumption #3: People (functional experts) are great leaders and managers.

The types of knowledge and skill – or expertise - needed in a business are best determined by the very nature of the value the organization needs to deliver. Functional expertise does not guarantee good management or leadership skills are present. Leadership is about managing change, while management is about creating sustainability.

---

ex·pert */'ek͵spərt/*

noun: a person who has a comprehensive and authoritative **knowledge of or skill in a particular area.**

"a financial expert"

ex·per·tise */ekspər'tēz, ͵ekspər'tēs/*

noun: expert skill or knowledge in a field

Definitions from Oxford Languages

The Peter Principle

How do people traditionally rise into management and leadership positions in an organization?

The norm is to promote an expert who is highly effective in a field solely based on expertise in that field, and there is often little assessment of the capability to manage or lead people.

There is also an added assumption that they will be the best at designing how their organization will run because of their functional prowess.

We refer to this type of advancement as the Peter Principle, a management theory concept formulated by Laurence J Peter in 1968. He says that "the selection of a candidate for a position is based on their current role, rather than abilities relevant to the intended role."

Thus, promotion of employees stops once they can no longer perform effectively. In other words: "managers rise to the level of their incompetence."

A top-down functionally based hierarchy enforces the Peter Principle as we consider functional expertise over leadership competency.

Adapted from Wikipedia

It is rare to find true leaders in traditional organizations, as hierarchical structures deter the behavior or development of them.

Assumption #4. People (functional experts) know how to best design a business

The Misapplication of Expertise

Simply put, organizations hire functional experts and assume that they will do two things:

1) Provide strong leadership

2) Enhance Organizational Design and Performance

Functional Expertise does not ensure sound strategy or execution; it only ensures that we have an expert inside a *function* of the organization. A financial expert learns the process of accounting, and that does not mean they will create practical accounting processes across the organization.

Consider which scenario will deliver better outcomes faster with less effort:

1. Experts working a poorly designed process.

2. Novices working a well-engineered process.

Notice your immediate inclination to expect an experts' ability to trump the power of process. Let us look at a few processes designed by functional experts, and you can decide for yourself which of the above scenarios is best.

Case Study: Financial Department with Inadequate Financial Processes

---

Admission: *It is when I took a similar Finance project on in my next organization, which was to streamline the budgeting process to reduce cycle time, that it became clear to me that budgeting added little value.*

The Problem:

The leadership team experienced consistent lateness of financial reporting. The finance team was frustrated as well, as they repeatedly needed to spend long days at the end of every month, and into the start of the next, working to complete the reporting. The team also complained about the elevated level of corrections necessary every month.

My Approach:

We formed a cross-functional team to include budget owners and representatives from relative functions in the finance department to analyze the financial reporting process using business process engineering methods.

The Findings:

The reporting process consisted of excessive approvals thought to satisfy regulatory requirements which added three days to process. The team experienced a 30% error rate in expense justification received from budget owners and had difficulty matching these to the Chart of Accounts. Correcting each of these errors typically took 1-5 days. The process lacked feedback loops from budget owners to ensure that there was continuous improvement in communication and quality. Also lacking was instruction and definition for budget owners in the organization to send simple and clear information that the finance department could use.

The Results:

Within two weeks, the team had developed and implemented well-defined standard responses for budget owners, with these changes thankfully received across the organization.

- Error rates dropped from 30% to 2%.

- We eliminated five approval cycles by utilizing data to validate work instead of approvals. The sixth approval cycle, formerly three layers of approvals became one approval (a true regulatory requirement) designed to mitigate delays, dramatically shortening the reporting cycle without being detrimental to quality.

- Month end financial reports became consistently available to the organization on the third business day of the following month. Staff no longer spent long days in an all-out push to have the reporting completed.

- Newer members of the team noted that they were finding it easier to come up to speed on the new process. All stakeholders found the new process far easier to follow.

The finance team in this example would be the first to tell you that the old process was not working well. And re-engineering this process to work for the business had nothing to do with instructing finance experts how to perform accounting or generate financial reports. Instead, re-engineering this process had everything to do with designing how financial tasks could be satisfied with a practical company-wide shared process.

Case Study: Utilities Engineering Department with Inadequate Engineering Processes

---

The Problem:

Leadership set an arbitrary goal to reduce by 10 days the average time to completion.

My manager's approach:

A Director of Engineering with no prior experience had recently attended training in basic business process engineering practices (for 4 days) and given a major process improvement activity to lead. He facilitated a 5-day event, only including managers from his department, where they created a process map that represented the current state as they knew it, notated with issues known or perceived by them.

My Approach:

I physically walked through the design and installation processes in multiple locations across the country, noting issues discovered only by watching people work and listening to their concerns.

The Findings:

Besides localized issues, I began to hear consistent complaints from workers about incessant process changes as well as lack of training and of usable information available in the suite of disjoined systems that they had access to. No two engineers worked the same process. A flawed assumption by management was that upon receiving the new procedures, workers had time to fully read and understand all the changes. Nothing was further from the truth.

As I watched people performing work, I noted how disjointed their work was as compared to how easy the policy makers thought it was. Each policy focused on how to use a technology system instead of how to work the process.

There were only a few measures in place to ensure process adherence, so management knew not of the fact that the outputs from the process varied greatly – they only focused on average time to completion.

Upon completing statistical analysis on average time to completion data, I found the distribution to be bimodal, indicating that there were factors that allowed faster completion for certain types of projects. I recommended measuring each group of projects separately to better uncover the root cause of delays. Management stuck with measuring only the average of all projects under one metric.

Managing by budget had driven the engineering department to outsource 50% of its work. Now company employees were spending up to 50% of their time overseeing and approving work performed by contractors. While I was analyzing engineering processes, the consistent complaint I heard from engineers was that they wanted to just be engineers! There was no training or guidelines offered by the company for overseeing contractors.

The disconnects in communication had created many added coordination meetings to keep projects on track. I calculated the number of hours spent on coordination meetings across the engineering department – we were wasting 120 FTE hours (the equivalent to 120 people in the design and installation process doing nothing but unnecessary work every hour of every day).

The Results:

After the Director had been leading a team of managers to improve the process for several months, they had not achieved any improvements in average completion time.

I presented several opportunities to remove non-value-added activity from the process and create a better customer experience as well as to improve average completion time by 20 days. These facts were unknown to engineering managers, the director, and the EVP of Engineering until I presented my findings.

The Director stole my findings as his analysis and our process engineering group included in the next downsizing.

This company's customers were going to continue to experience delays and frustration, and people working in the engineering department that had suffered for years were going to continue to suffer, because I, as someone that had only been in the business for 5 months, could not know more about process issues than tenured managers.

Poor, but natural, assumption in a hierarchical and functional expert-focused world.

Assumption #5: Technology will always improve how People work.

Some businesses exist to supply technology. Organizations also use technologies, be they mechanical, scientific, or informational. The technology that I refer to here is information technology. The ultimate purpose of technology is to automate that which is mind-numbing, repetitive, difficult, or when high speed or higher precision than a human can deliver is desired. There is a strong mainstream belief currently that automation is always better. This is not necessarily the case. Automating processes is not the ultimate solution to delivering value and can in fact prevent the delivery of value.

Many professionals report how technology hampers process with great cost expended for resources with loss of business agility. As a consumer, how often have you called Customer Service and the representative genuinely wants to help but must inform you that "our system does not allow us to do that."

The way to design Technology is for flexibility, but I have never seen an IT system designed with all the business rules (factors, decisions) embedded at the start of the workflows. This the easiest way to allow the business to change processes without major reprogramming. The typical way technology gathers requirements is by interviewing people who are currently working weak processes to describe what they currently do, and that is the information captured for the software development teams. Technology development and implementation problems ensue, as Invariably the old broken process becomes hard coded in that technology. Many business professionals report how technology hampers the organization, at great cost in resources and business agility.

Tim Gray, a supply chain expert, developed his own inexpensive supply chain management software after experiencing Enterprise Resource Planning (ERP) systems lack flexibility.

A popular mega system that many companies use cripples the ability to analyze purchase potential, only allowing for one price point per part or product. Based on best practice processes and knowing that successful organizations are flexible ones, his software allows management to change the system's business rules as desired to adapt to changing times. Tim averages 461% ROI for his clients.

(With permission from www.prophitsystems.com)

Chapter 6

The #1 Reason Startups Fail and All Organizations Underperform

*"There's an old man there from the old world
Calls all his customers by name...
These days a man makes you somethin'
and you never see his face"*
— Chosen lyrics from Sunset Grill, by Don Henley & Danny Kortchmar

Knowing how we arrived to believing status quo practices work will help in creating a new outlook for the future. Here is a short story depicting a typical business formed prior to the industrial revolution.

John was a successful cobbler who made durable, comfortable, and affordable shoes. John managed the buying of materials, measuring, making, and selling of shoes to his customers.

Many of his customers shared with others about how wonderful John's shoes were.

After John's death, his son Sam continued to provide amazing shoes with the same great service. Why is it that Sam could deliver the same quality shoes as his father John? John had many more years of experience (expertise) than Sam, but he had learned from his father *a proven method* for crafting shoes. Our natural belief is that only Sam's expertise makes him good at his trade. The truth is that Sam's Father trained him on a *series of proven processes, and he is successful because he follows them.*

We inherit processes, not expertise.

It is not people or technology that are the primary factors to deliver value in an organization. People will come and people will go. Technology will come and technology will go. What continues to deliver value even when people and technology change?

Process. The process is always there.

People and Technology ENABLE Processes.

Process is the dimension taken for granted and it is all we have in the end - we would best take care of it.

Welcome to working in a 3-dimensional world.

THE FUTURE OF WORKING TOGETHER

"It's not about working harder; it's about working the system. It's not about who puts in the most work, but who knows the best areas to focus on. With thorough inspection and reflection, we can determine the weakest links of our ideas and processes. Don't forget to pause, examine, and work more effectively."
                              - Evan Spiegel, CEO, Snapchat

The Future of Working TogetherSM is what is possible when we design organizations to be value focused and synergetic. Here I introduce The Future of Working Together ModelSM to embrace a new organizational Focus, Structure, and Mindset that can end common organizational problems and allow for a powerful new future to emerge.

---

fu·ture /ˈfyo͞oCHər/

noun: the time or a period of time following the moment of speaking or writing.

Similar: time to come, **what lay/lies ahead**

adjective: at a later time; going or **likely to happen** *or exist.*

"The needs of future generations"

Similar: ensuing, succeeding, **upcoming**

---

working together

Synergy. *alliance*. *joint effort*. **harmony**. *team effort*. **teaming**.

Adapted from www.thesaurus.com

Chapter 7

Working in a 3-Dimensional World

"We should work ON our process, not the outcome of our processes."
— W. Edwards Deming

"Process is the most powerful yet neglected dimension in business"
— Dawn Holly Johnson

---

proc·ess   /ˈprä͜ses, ˈprō͜ses/

noun: a series of actions or steps taken to achieve a particular end

*synonyms: procedure, operation, action, **activity**, exercise, **business**, job, task*

verb: performing a series of operations

Definitions from Oxford Languages

Everything we do is a process. Anything we provide to the world takes a process to deliver it.

What is the most neglected dimension in business? **Process.**

The Recipe

You birth a new idea – a new recipe. You work hard to develop the recipe to create a valuable offering for the world. You evaluate this concept to make sure it is not only practical, but that the marketplace is hungry for it. You develop a powerful recipe to produce your offering. With some sweat equity and funding, you are ready to cook!

You form a company and hire expert Chefs to lead various functions to produce your recipe.

And this is where the failure begins.

Various functional areas are each given a part of the recipe to produce. Each expert (Chef) makes a piece of the recipe, and each Chef can "improve" their piece of the recipe as they like. Over time, our Chefs begin to lose agreement on what the recipe should be and lose understanding of what made the recipe great in the first place, driving poor decision making and company underperformance. But these are award-winning Chefs! How can this be so? Any great Chef will tell you that a culinary masterpiece comes from fine tuning the recipe.

But our traditionally designed and operated company has allowed leaders to change the recipe method and ingredients for their area without consulting other leaders, so our recipe is no longer what it was, with everyone involved expecting a different product outcome based on the piece of the recipe they understand and support in making.

Now the company is not delivering quality meals on time, Chefs begin to blame people and technology. Having invested much in people and technology to make our culinary delight, then it must be people and technology that keep us from making it great!

"I need a new Cuisinart," proclaims one Chef.

"We need new ovens!" insists another.

"We need to retrain our people; they need to follow the recipe!" yells a third Chef.

Now we are spending precious capital on training, firing, and hiring people, and buying the next great technology. Yet from all of this effort, we experience little to no improvement in company performance or in delivering delicious meals, so we believe we must invest even more in people and technology - and the cycle continues.

The result of organizations not controlling processes (the recipe) and trusting functional experts (Chefs) to make the best decisions for their functional areas is as follows:

For startups - they burn through capital faster than planned. Fifty percent of startups fail within the first 4 years. I have researched many articles expounding on the reasons startups fail and these explanations all boil down to two things: a weak value proposition and lack of proper funding. Most startups spend capital faster than predicted by wasteful practices driven by status quo thinking and not accounted for in financial predictions.

For established businesses / organizations – as leaders continue to follow status quo practices, the organization veers farther and farther away with growth to reaching its maximum potential, and the larger organizations grow, the more difficult to align people, driving a negative culture.

In healthcare, medical error is now the third leading cause of death in the United States, with this statistic underreported. There is opportunity to have patient-centric processes designed across the healthcare system.

For government – raising of taxes and inflationary printing of money is necessary to cover exorbitant inefficiencies.

Ever heard of the saying "This is a recipe for disaster?"

Consider that in traditional organizations the recipe has evolved, in silos, over time, and no longer has integrity. The recipe will never deliver what we need it to. This is the traditional design of organizations at work. We start with an amazing recipe that produces an excellent product. As the business grows, we divide the recipe by functional expertise and hire consultants when we fail to improve on the recipe. Another famous saying comes to mind "Too many cooks spoil the broth."

Just because someone is an expert in a particular area, they may not know what is best to change in the overall recipe. Just because we implement different technology does not mean that we will deliver better on our overall intended outcome.

Everything we do in life is a process. Everything. Pay attention to the process and you will begin to reap great rewards.

It is the combination of three dimensions that produce a valuable product or service:

1. A good recipe is a list of accurately measured ingredients, clear instructions on how to prepare each ingredient and how and when to combine them in the proper order (a measured proven process.)
2. People with the right capabilities for their role follow the recipe (the right people contributing to, and knowing the value of, the measured proven process).
3. The right tools (technology) for the job are available to best produce the recipe (enable the process).

Following the recipe (process) is what has us deliver a predictable result, so the recipe (process) had better be well-defined, repeatable, measurable, and controlled.

It takes focusing on all three dimensions: Process, People, and Technology - and in that order to establish a Wildly Successful Enterprise.

"But people are important! How can you put them in second place?" The answer I have for this question is this: if you do not design workable, effective processes to produce value, you really do not care about your employees (or your customers). Process is not what we traditionally focus on in business. We assume the experts we hire will design great processes. But they are not process experts, they are functional experts.

There is a proven way to design organizations so that the value delivery process is naturally the focus of the organization.

People and technology come and go; process is always there.

Everything we do is a process. For example, organizational safety professionals will train personnel on a process for performing a simple task: picking up a box to not cause injury. Our daily routines are a process, we drive in a traffic system following various processes, even turning on the television is a process. Think of showing a child for the first time how to turn on a television and choose what to watch. You show them the steps (activities) to conduct turning the television on and selecting the desired media and programs (outcome)! *We take processes for granted because we are always following them.*

Defining organizational processes

I refer to main delivery processes as *core processes*, analogous to the large branches of a tree that deliver nourishment to produce fruit. The fundamental activities for delivering value to customers takes place in the core process(es) or value streams. Value streams are the end-to-end processes that deliver a product or service directly to the customer. Some examples of elements of a value stream would be an online shopping portal, assembly of a product, marketing content, providing a service, and/or onsite installation of a product. Ideally, the primary focus of your organization is to deliver the best value by keeping the value streams healthy. In functionally based hierarchical organizational structures the core process is not the focus. Look at any traditional organizational chart. Can you discern the core processes? the support processes? The answer is no. But we do know who reports to whom!

Make value easy for your customers to experience

Have you ever contacted a company call center to report an issue and the customer service representative would like to help you, but they do not have the authority, or the technology system will not allow them to correct it? Does this leave you frustrated? It should. The design of most process helps an organization, not its customers. As traditional processes grow organically department by department, these processes will lack focus on what the customer values.

What if the process design itself allowed for flexibility and a company representative could choose to manage your request? You would be delighted! Value delivery organizations design their processes to be flexible, creating efficiency while supplying the best value possible to the customer.

Southwest Airlines is a fantastic business model that provides flexibility for Customers (and the people working there are happier too!)

When a life event occurs and you need to change your flight, you can call them or visit their website and change flights quickly. You can reallocate your flight funds toward your newly scheduled flight without penalty, and this is possible up to 10 minutes before the flight is due to depart. There is no cost to you for this change, and why should there be? Life happens.

Southwest Airlines has designed its ticketing processes with focus on what customers want— hassle free changes. There is negligible risk to the airline for simply swapping your seat on one flight for a seat on another. A seat sold is a seat sold – why should it matter what flight?

Yet other airlines charge upward of $150 for you to change reservations. That is simply an airline charging you for a life event - 5 minutes of their time (zero if you change the ticket online) - and comes from a scarcity attitude. The mindset with traditional airlines is to charge their customers fees when inevitable life changes occur to pay for inefficient corporate structure and overhead.

Structure your organization to be nimble enough to change with your customers' needs and it will thrive. Is your organization supplying what customers desire, or what leaders desire? Unless you design the end-to-end process to deliver value, your organization is not truly customer focused.

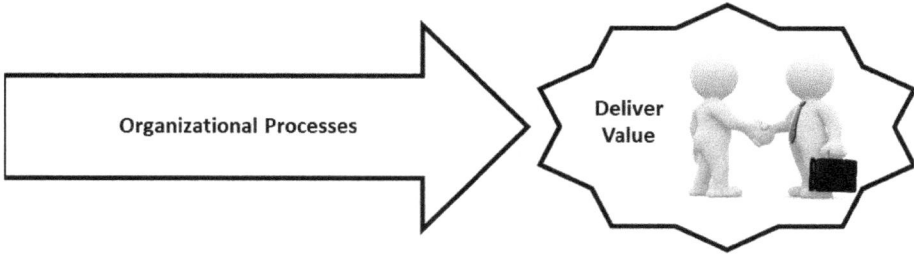

Processes are the primary conduit to deliver your value proposition to the world

---

The 3D Value Model

"Process, people and technology all have to work together and are interdependent. These three dimensions of a successful organization start with the right process and that is something that I think a lot of people, as they start a business, don't even look at."
— Michael Gibson

We need a new model for organizations that incorporates the power of process while best aligning people and technology. It is time we worked together in a 3-dimensional world.

The Three Dimensions of Value Generation

1. Design Processes to deliver value
2. Assign People to steward the process
3. Align Technology to enable the process

The Three Outcomes of Value Realization

1. Organizational Alignment and Harmony
2. Outstanding Customer, Shareholder and Employee Satisfaction
3. Optimal Performance and Profit

This is the winning model - working in a 3-dimensional world. Working in all three dimensions is a new paradigm that, when adopted, will accelerate performance for any organization. This is why I titled my company 3D Value Group – all three dimensions are critical for any endeavors' success. Designing organizations with processes that deliver value to customers should be job number one. Why else are you in business but to deliver value to your customers?

It is our value delivery process that we need to organize ourselves around. Organizing (and re-organizing) businesses around people degrades our processes; then we apply technology on top of the mess.

We deliver value through our processes, not through our organizational chart.

Create a strong core process based on a thorough understanding of what customers value. When people align to value delivery processes, everyone has the same priority because their focus is on delivering value. There are no politics needed to convince one leader to change their approach to help improve other areas of the business. With aligning everyone to deliver value, there is a clear purpose and direction to focus on the same outcomes. In turn, this alignment naturally creates strong collaboration and teamwork and happier customers and employees. Only then can Technology meaningfully enable the delivery process. Our culture shifts to one of empowerment.

In Part 2, I will show you how to engineer and manage your business for high performance. You are able to create a well-engineered organization without needed to be an engineer. You do not need to understand aerodynamics, like I do, to get on a plane and fly to a destination, and you do not need an engineering background to create a Wildly Successful Enterprise – I have provided the design for you.

When engineering a physical structure, you must consider the pull of gravity.

Allow value delivery to be your organization's gravity – your pull towards a new focus.

Chapter 8
Future Focus

**"Our research reveals that, on average, 95% of [an organizations']
employees are unaware of or do not understand its strategy. If the
employees who are closest to customers and who work processes
that create value are unaware of the strategy, they surely cannot
help the organization implement it effectively."**

- Harvard Business Review

What CEOs want is an easy to manage, profitable and sustainably growing
business that adapts easily to changing times. What employees want is to enjoy
their work and feel like they are contributing. This is entirely possible when you
change **organizational Focus, Structure, and Mindset.**

Here we will address what focus to adopt to improve organizational
performance. To gain clarity on what to focus on, refer to the very definition of
what a business is.

What Is a Business?

*The definition of a business is an organization or enterprising entity
engaged in commercial, industrial, or professional activities.*

*The term "business" also refers to the organized efforts and activities
of individuals to produce and sell goods and services for profit.*

Adapted from Invesopedia.com

As mentioned in the quote at the start of this chapter, if 95% of employees on average do not understand the organization's strategy (or purpose), how well can it be delivering on that purpose?

---

or·gan·i·za·tion   /ôrgənəˈzāSH(ə)n/

*noun: **an organized body of people with a particular purpose.***

*Similar: company, operation, corporation, institution, group, **society***

Definitions from Oxford Languages

If a business organizes efforts and activities of individuals to produce and sell goods and services for profit, it **should be well structured to systemically deliver on a particular purpose.**

---

or·gan·ized   /ˈôrgəˌnīzd/

*adjective: **1. arranged in a systematic way, especially on a large scale. 2. to deal with things efficiently.***

*Similar: **Well-ordered, efficient, systemic, structured***

Definitions from Oxford Languages

What is the purpose of your organization? Purpose motivates and creates, trust, alignment for the organization. What assures financial viability of an organization is that the purpose aligns with what potential customers value.

---

pur·pose   /ˈpərpəs/

noun: the reason for which something is done or created or for which something exists.

*Similar: **motivation, cause, reason,** justification, intention, aim, **objective,** goal, **value,** result*

verb: have as one's intention or objective.

Similar: intend, aim, plan, design

Every organization is meant to deliver on a purpose, hopefully a well-intended purpose. Purpose creates energy and motivation, increases performance, and defines everything your organization stands for – employees, customers, communities, and the world. Having a meaningful purpose makes a difference for any organization - including doubling employee retention rates.

88% of those surveyed would take a 15% pay cut to work in an organization that shared their values.

– Excerpt from "CAUSE! A business strategy for standing out in a sea of sameness" – by Jackie and Kevin Freiberg

---

Developing and keeping top talent comes depends on organizational design, as a design can create or defy healthy growth and development. If people feel valued, and know they are delivering value, then they grow, develop, and stay. Traditional organizations by very design do not create environments that are helpful for people to grow and develop; the best talent leave because they are tired of bureaucracy, politics, and lack of appreciation, and the people that remain comprise a dangerously complacent workforce.

What value does your organization provide?

"Price is what you pay. Value is what you get."

- Warren Buffet

---

val·ue /valyoo/

noun: the regard that something is held to deserve; **the importance, worth or usefulness of something.**

Synonyms: worth, usefulness, advantage, benefit, gain, profit, good, help

Definitions from Oxford Languages

Any success comes from delivering VALUE. Please take a moment to ponder this question:

What VALUE does your organization deliver to the world?

Really contemplate this question and write down your answer.

Now, independently ask each member of your leadership team the same question. Record their individual answers. Finally, ask a sample of employees this same question. A good sample size is twenty-five or more employees per one thousand. Ask all employees if your organization has less than 25 employees. **Have any two people you asked agreed on the value your organization delivers?** It is likely that this is not the case.

It is simply not practical to improve organizational performance unless everyone focuses on delivering the same result. Better decisions are a natural occurrence if the focus of everyone is on delivering the same VALUE, and the **definition of VALUE decided by all stakeholders**. You may argue that you measure customer and employee satisfaction but measuring satisfaction in no way defines what is possible.

There is a new wave of CEOs that publicly committed to changing the traditionally myopic view of focusing solely on Shareholder value (focus on the Balance Sheet) to an all-inclusive focus on Stakeholder value. Stakeholders of an organization, in addition to shareholders, include customers, employees, suppliers, partners, regulatory agencies, and communities affected by what the organization generates (products and by-products of the organizations existence). I believe we should also include greater societal, economic, and environmental impacts when evaluating delivering value.

The Business Roundtable, a group of Chief Executive Officers of 181 major U.S. corporations, issued a statement with a new definition of the purpose of a corporation, dropping the age-old notion that their corporations will no longer function primarily to serve their shareholders and maximize profits. The new focus is to invest in employees, deliver value to customers, deal ethically with suppliers, and support outside communities.

Adapted from https://www.cnbc.com/2019/08/19/the-ceos-of-nearly-two-hundred-companies-say-shareholder-value-is-no-longer-their-main-objective.html

---

I was happy to hear that a large group of corporate America CEOs committed to changing their focus from shareholder to *stakeholder value*. Being a CEO has traditionally been more about what is in it for them than making the company, or people working in it, whole for the long term. Unfortunately, many of these CEOs are not following the agreement.

It is no surprise that, over the decades in which the consensus set in that a chief executive's main job was to create value for their shareholders, boards began adding ever more stock to CEOs' compensation packages. This, the refrain went, was the way to match up the interests [of CEOs to shareholders].

Yet a couple of strange things have happened in the two years since the US Business Roundtable made its symbolic break with shareholder primacy.

First, the investors [shareholders] have begun voting against CEOs' compensation packages in ever larger numbers.

Second, executive incentives have remained overwhelmingly focused on shareholder outcomes, even as they have been busy professing what fine stakeholder capitalists they are.

So, the way companies now pay their top officers is not satisfying shareholders while undermining executives' credibility as guardians of other stakeholders' interests.

This week, a study spanning seven European countries found an 18 per cent increase this year in shareholders dissenting overpay resolution.

In the US, protests over executives' rewards have hit a record high, with once placid institutions baulking at the $230M GE gave CEO Larry Culp and the $155m Bobby Kotick took home for running Activision Blizzard.

You do not have to wonder how much empathy a CEO earning nine digits has with employees and other stakeholders barely scratching a living. Yet it is still startling that three-quarters of investors now think that executive pay is simply too high, as a recent London Business School survey found.

In a controversial analysis of Business Roundtable members' actions since signing 2019's stakeholder pledge, two Harvard Law School

> *academics last month found that none had yet tied directors' compensation to stakeholders' interests.*
>
> *But those stakeholder metrics which boards have adopted typically focus on annual bonuses and put little of the CEOs total compensation at risk. Investors suspect that boards are simply adding complexity to already conveniently impenetrable packages.*
>
> It is not just CEOs who should benefit from equity ownership by Andrew Edgecliffe-Johnson, Financial Times

---

What CEOs need to know is how to create equity through delivering stakeholder value. Timing is everything, and there is now a momentum behind what I am proposing in these pages – an acceleration towards a new future of working together.

Changing your focus to stakeholder value is one thing, and it is paramount, but how do you transform an organization of people with traditional mindsets to quickly evolve to adopting new ways of working? You *adopt the structure and mindset* of the organization to be value focused as discussed in the next chapters.

Define your organization's value proposition

> *"A customer is the most important visitor on our premises.*
> *He is not dependent on us; we are dependent on him.*
> *He is not an interruption of our work; he is the purpose of it.*
> *He is not an outsider of our business; he is part of it.*
> *We are not doing him a favour by serving him.*
> *He is doing us a favour by giving us the opportunity to do so."*
> *- Mahatma Ghandi*

Ask your potential customers and other stakeholders what is valuable about your products and services. How great *you* believe your products and services are does not matter. The best way to research the value of your offerings is to ask *potential* customers about the value your products and services can potentially provide to them. Your current customers are already accustomed to your products or services and will not always be a reliable source for defining customer value. However, understanding your current customers experience of using your product or service is imperative. All stakeholders, employees, stockholders, suppliers, the communities you serve, all expect value from your organization. Ask them what that value is that they expect.

Healthcare Providers are Health Insurance Stakeholders

While working to improve the Provider onboarding process in a Fortune 100 Health Insurance Company, I had a conversation with a Provider Call Center lead.

As she expounded on their latest focus - to reduce the number of call transfers in the call center - I asked why this effort was important.

She responded that call transfers drove higher operational costs.

I was not surprised by her response. The departments' focus was on reducing call transfers to reduce costs to the call center. The focus was on how to make department budget issues dissipate, not on eliminating problems Healthcare Providers encountered while working with us.

During this discussion, there was no mention of Healthcare Provider needs or wants, or about why needing to call in with an issue in the first place was necessary. Furthermore, there was no thought to how these problems impacted insurance customers. Healthcare Providers and insurance customers are the key stakeholders in the health insurance industry.

My inclination was to uncover how the value delivery system was failing; to determine what was causing Healthcare Providers to call us with a problem in the first place.

But the call center operational budget was the focus of the effort, not on supplying value to Healthcare Providers or to insured customers.

And please realize that in some cases, mistakes in identifying and processing insurance coverage benefits result in delays to care and sometimes cause unnecessary death.

The best way to prove your value proposition is to supply an unbiased explanation of your products and services and ask for their critique. It is easy to lead people to the answer you want, so be careful to ask questions that stakeholders can freely answer. I have seen many surveys that ask leading questions and supply multiple choice answers; here you are leading the witness. You will gain amazing insights in allowing people to really think about and allow for unrestrained comment on what would be of value to them to use your products and services, if you ask potential customers and stakeholders what they would ideally expect to experience with your products or services. Take this value feedback and incorporate it into your product and/or service designs and processes.

There are proven methods for gathering and understanding customer requirements (wants and needs) and translating them into robust product and service designs. My favorite method is Design for Six Sigma, also known as the House of Quality, a method widely used in Aerospace and Automotive industries to ensure reliability. I have used this method in software development and healthcare delivery processes with fantastic results.

Value Proposition

A value proposition is a statement that denotes the value your organization can provide to a potential customer.

A Value Proposition should answer the question: "If I am your ideal customer, why should I buy from you instead of any of your competitors?"

Most marketing professionals struggle with defining the value proposition because their organization:

1. Has not identified it.

2. Does not clearly express it.

3. Is not testing or measuring it.

Adapted from https://www.kunocreative.com/blog/good-value-proposition-examples

---

Not clearly communicating, and focusing everyone on, your organization's value proposition is a top reason for underperformance. Simply leaving it up to your marketing team to develop your value proposition is a huge mistake. Define your value proposition(s) with all your stakeholders, and then ensure everyone associated with your organization knows and aligns with these value statements. **Imagine if the value proposition of your business is so well-defined, so clear to everyone, that potential customers, employees, and suppliers gravitate to it – all stakeholders embrace it. Imagine the focus that would create!** Having all stakeholders embracing your organization's value proposition delivers these benefits:

- Common focus and natural alignment for everyone associated with the enterprise
- Developing trust with customers, employees, and other stakeholders
- Everyone will make better decisions
- Utilizing less time and resource delivering your products and services to customers
- Having the ability to offer higher quality at a lower price point
- Simplified management of the organization

Traditionally, only the marketing department develops a value proposition. Knowing your value proposition is Marketing 101. The problem with this is that one department decides what to announce as your value proposition, and it is flawed in that the advertised value proposition is unknown to the rest of the organization.

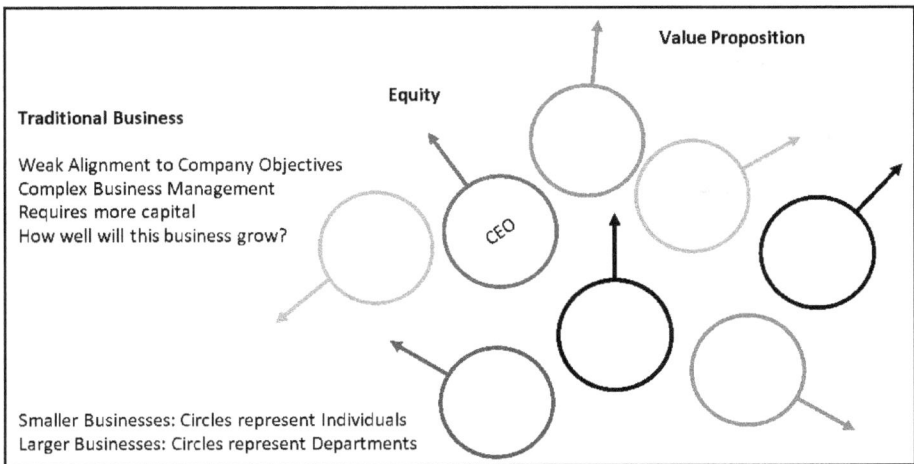

Lack of focus in a Traditional Organization

It is commonplace to have sales and marketing personnel make promises to potential customers that the rest of the organization are unaware of and often not set up to fulfill on. There is a universal disconnect between Sales and Marketing and Operational departments in every traditional organization. Disconnects in focus create problems that negatively affect financials.

Focus on Value and Financial Success Follows

"The new way of business? Communities...be with them, open the walls and succeed together."

– Hamdi Ulukaya, CEO of Chobani

"Spreadsheets are lazy"

Hamdi Ulukaya, CEO of Chobani, who coined the term Anti-CEO Playbook[3] speaks about how the primary focus of being a leader is about taking care of people and not only will the financials work out, but the community will thrive.

"The new way of business is that business, not government, is in the best position to make a change in all cultural challenges. Today's CEO playbook"- is placating to the corporate boards and not the customer, yet the customer is the reason for business existence.

3 Adapted from https://www.ted.com/talks/hamdi_ulukaya_the_anti_ceo_playbook

---

Interestingly, if you empower employees in any organization to collaborate on the design of processes to deliver value, they will enthusiastically jump to task. Empower people to ask for the resources (technical, human, material, infrastructure) they need to make the process supply higher value. Have everyone focused on the customer value you are providing.

To measure value, you need to focus on the ability of your organization to deliver it. When evaluating processes in traditional organizations, I am always amazed at the number of financial processes that exist. Traditional organizations spend an exorbitant amount of effort measuring financials, performing financial forecasting, and planning and controlling budgets and these efforts take precedence over measuring value delivery and process health.

Focusing on the Value Proposition strengthens organizational alignment

The following recommended practices are fundamental to transforming an organization to become, and remain, focused on delivering stakeholder value.

The Future of Working Together Practice #1: Process Control

Replaces the traditional practice of Budget Control

"85% of the reasons for failure are deficiencies in the systems and processes rather than the employee. The role of management is to change the process rather than badgering individuals to do better.
— W. Edwards Deming

What you measure, you control. Focus on the budget and you are working hard to control estimated income and expenses while impeding performance, innovation, value delivery, and damaging livelihoods.

Since processes are the conduits to delivering value, we instead want to focus on ensuring they are healthy, in control and delivering value.

A process in control *is a process changed only when a proven and sustainable improvement solution is available.*

Lack of Process Control is like this:

Imagine that your organizational value proposition is to generate a radio broadcast at 101.5 FM, and every department has access to tuning dials to adjust the frequency however they decide.

Department A turns the dial to a higher frequency, Department B a lower frequency, Department C a much higher frequency and so on. What are your chances of the organization broadcasting consistently at 101.5 FM without control as to who can turn a dial and when?

Designing healthy measurable controlled processes is what I was originally trained to do as a quality and process engineer as the aerospace industry embraced continuous improvement back in the 1990's. To this day most leaders do not understand the importance of process control, as hierarchical structure takes the focus away from the delivery process and a quick-fixing mindset creates the need for constant changes to the process. Process experts know how to design healthy processes to deliver value and keep them in control, and functional experts do not.

Unlike some in my profession, I am not a purist – I am a pragmatist. I am not proposing any process improvement method. Every method has practices to apply when and where they make sense.

Lean continuous improvement seeks to improve every process in your company by focusing on enhancing the activities that generate the most value for your customer while removing as many waste activities as possible.

https://kanbanize.com/lean-management/improvement/what-is-continuous-improvement.

I mention the Lean method here to show that there exists an already defined value-focused accounting method that your organization can adapt to embrace focusing on process control instead of budget control.

Traditional Assumptions

- *Profit comes from full use of resources*

- *Control the business through detailed financial tracking*

- *Excess capacity is bad*

- *Direct labor is the most important conversion cost*

Lean Assumptions

- *Profit comes from delivering value as and when requested by Customers*

- *Control through continuous attention to improving the value delivery flow*

- *Excess capacity provides flexibility*

- *Cost is derived from impeding value delivery*

Adapted from https://www.slideshare.net/ahmad1957/ leanaccountingsample

---

There are ways to account for value delivery, most notable is the method of accounting for Lean. The following are comparisons of Traditional to Lean Accounting assumptions and measures.

Lean Accounting: *Applying concepts to drive waste out of the accounting function itself (which a prior case study was an example of)*

Accounting for Lean: *Modifying the accounting process to deliver information which promotes Lean (value delivery focused) behaviors.*

Traditional Measurements (Financial)

- *Labor efficiency & asset utilization*
- *Cost variance vs. standard*
- *Budget adherence*
- *Direct labor as % of sales*

Lean Measurements (Value Delivery Process)

- *Process and Activity Cycle Time*
- *Process Throughput*
- *First time quality*
- *Inventory turns (reduced backlogs)*
- *Value Delivery to Customer*
- *Value Stream health*

Adapted from https://www.slideshare.net/ahmad1957/leanaccountingsample

---

Focus on meeting the needs of the customer vs. meeting the needs of the budget. Always strive to meet the needs of the customer by developing a balance on what you measure and what you do. Putting most of the effort on measurement of financials disregards process value delivery to customers, employee growth and development, and other value contribution efforts.

When I perform observations of people working, it becomes clear that they do not understand the big picture of the end-to-end delivery process they work in or support. Due to this lack of awareness, people will make decisions based on their limited purview, and change processes and procedures without an understanding of the impact to other departments. In traditional organizations, it is common to find rework processes in play to correct upstream mistakes. I have removed entire large processes from organizations because those processes were 100% rework, and I have done this without the consequence of downsizing, allowing for more people to help improve the process.

A Note on Business Process Engineering

You are an expert at what you do, and to develop strong value focus you need to create healthy value delivery processes. To do this, you will need Business Process Engineering experts to help you. Business Process Engineers (BPEs) partner with functional experts to find, create, measure, and manage powerful processes. I supply guidelines on the attributes of a good BPE in Chapter 11, because like every area of expertise, some BPEs demonstrate a higher aptitude than others.

The Future of Working Together Practice #2: Always the right size

---

Replaces the traditional practice of Downsizing

"There is nothing so useless as doing efficiently that which should not be done at all."

- *Jez Humble*

"Right-sized organizations need not downsize."

- *Dawn Holly Johnson*

Value focused organizations avoid complexity, non-value-added effort, and expenditure that organic growth creates and therefore naturally minimize overhead (picture a perfectly pruned tree). Adopting value delivery centric organizational structure (Chapter 9) and a collaborative, data driven problem solving mindset (Chapter 10) to maintain value focus produces, except for the exception of catastrophe, an organization that never requires downsizing. Even in the case of disruptive innovation, The Future of Working Together Model allows for organizations to be naturally adaptive and innovative.

The practice of downsizing becomes OBSOLETE.

The Future of Working Together Practice #3: Merging Process, Technology and Culture

---

Replaces the traditional practice of not measuring Merger and Acquisition (M&A) impact

---

"If you cannot describe what you are doing as a process, you do not know what you are doing."
— W. Edwards Deming

The true total cost and impact of traditional mergers and acquisitions is unknown, as typically only current financial worth is important. Once the consolidation of Balance Sheets of the merged companies is complete, all efforts to integrate cultures, processes, and technology systems lose priority. Traditional mergers interrupt the delivery of that value by dismantling key processes.

When we acquire a new product line, value-based organizations are far easier to manage in a merger or acquisition in that you already have aligned the organization to delivering value, so adding another product or service is easy to conduct. It is likely that the organization you are gaining is not value-focused or process-based, so it is imperative to define that organizations core processes, engineer those process for high performance and then incorporate those processes into the process-centric structure we will cover in the next chapter.

The Future of Working Together Practice #4: Accountability

Replaces the traditional practice of arbitrary goals and leadership bonuses
"I believe that when you share success, it grows."

– Hamdi Ulukaya, CEO, Chobani

There is an opportunity to drive accountability through the measurement of value generation. Everyone needs to be accountable for ensuring the organization delivers value and that the value proposition reflects current market trends. Goals and incentives become value-contribution-based with everyone in the organization rewarded for the part they play in organizational performance improvement. There are a few CEOs today that have realized the power in sharing the wealth – they are happier, and their job is easier, as the entire organization focuses on delivering value.

Recall the definition of an organization: a group of people brought together to deliver on a purpose. If everyone has incentive to deliver on the same purpose, amazing results happen. The easiest way to drive accountability is to make work activities transparent and make it worthwhile for people to perform activities. If everyone in the organization is accountable for delivering value, and the value delivery process is transparent (measured with activities well defined), then should anyone not focus on delivering value, the action would become immediately obvious, allowing for self-correction and/or process correction. Besides human resources, all focus all company resources on making delivery processes healthier.

Processes must be measurable so that you can continue to make them healthier and the performance of them more transparent for the benefit of all. Just like your doctor will measure blood pressure, pulse, weight, run blood tests, and ask about any negative symptoms you are experiencing, so must you measure to diagnose issues with your processes. Making data driven decisions is critical, yet not the norm in traditional organizations. Accurate and meaningful measurement of your business and value delivery processes is necessary to make good decisions.

Meaningful process measurements are typically non-existent in traditional processes created by functional experts. To give you an idea of the impact, consider that every year, over 250,000 people die in the United States alone due to medical error. Right away you are thinking medical error is about expert error. Measurement drives accountability. I surmise that most medical error is due to poorly designed and measured processes – they lack accountability. The medical error death rate in the United States is equivalent to the loss of human life due to the terrorist attacks that occurred on September 11, 2001, *happening every week.*

Casualties of the September 11 attacks

During the September 11, 2001, attacks, with 2,977 people killed, 19 hijackers committing murder–suicide, and more than 6,000 others injured. Of the 2,996 total deaths (including the terrorists), 2,763 occurred in the World Trade Center and the surrounding area, 189 at the Pentagon, and 44 in Pennsylvania [United Airlines Flight 93]. These deaths included 265 passengers on the four planes. The attacks stay the deadliest terrorist act in world history.

Excerpt From Wikipedia, the free encyclopedia

Please take 11 minutes to watch my YouTube video about Medical Error to hear how weak processes with lack of accountability can kill at https://bit.ly/3x1xlQo.

Changing focus is the first paradigm shift to make: a shift from focusing on the balance sheet to everyone being accountable for creating healthy, controlled processes focused on delivering the value proposition(s) for your organization.

Next, we will address organizational structure, the second paradigm shift: a shift from the traditional top-down functionally based hierarchy organizational structure to that of an efficient and effective value delivery structure.

Chapter 9

Future Organizational Structure

Leaders are responsible for creating an environment in which people feel they can be at their best."

— Simon Sinek

A CEO can declare to focus on stakeholder value and the organization is still functioning in the old paradigm. That momentum is hard to stop with traditional structure and mindset still in play. Due to design, traditional organizations do not focus on delivering value to customers. If we chose to do so, we would align our organizations to focus solely on value delivery to the customer instead of managing people in functional departments. Traditionally, it is uncommon to focus on value delivery yet ***the only way to win is to deliver outstanding value.***

There is no formal inclusion of the customer in a traditional organizational structure.

Value-Focused Organizational Structure

"The truth is incontrovertible. Malice may attack it, ignorance my deride it, but in the end...there it is."

— Sir Winston Churchill

Design your organization with the end in mind. The only way to deliver value is to focus on it, structure the organization to deliver it, and create a mindset to sustain it. For startups or smaller companies, changing your organizational structure will be an easier task. For mid-size or large organizations, it will take something, but you are already wasting exorbitant resources by reorganizing regularly to try to drive better outcomes, so why not reorganize one last time? You will never have to reorganize again. You may add new value streams with new products and services, but that is not reorganizing, that is scalable growth. I recommend larger companies re-engineer the organizational structure to focus on core end-to-end value delivery processes and move each process one-by-one over to a brand-new environment – known as a Greenfield - rather than trying to undo all the complexities (unravel the "spaghetti") created in the old environment – known as a Brownfield.

What we want to aim to achieve is an organizational structure that models this:

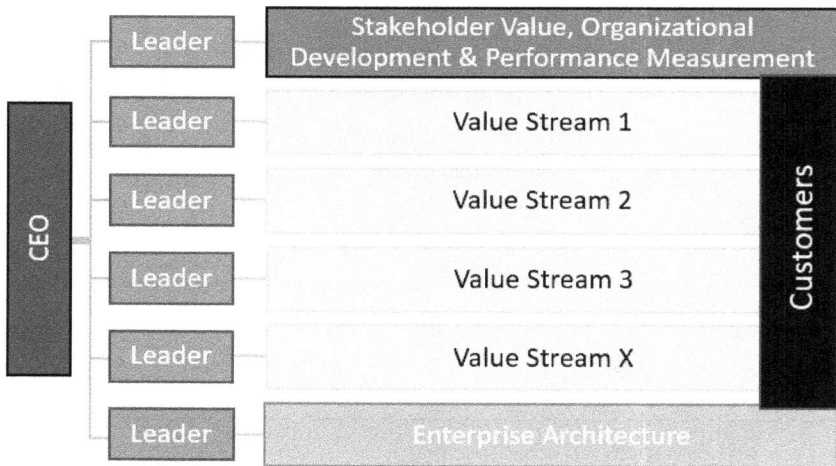

Value Delivery Organizational Structure Model

Consider each horizontal in the above illustration to be a Center of Excellence (COE).

The Stakeholder Value COE is subservient to the value streams as part of a process control mechanism. This COE focuses on activities that support and enable value streams to ensure the organization can best deliver value to all stakeholders.

Value Stream COEs are core value delivery processes that encompass a product and/or service families. Each value stream aligns with products and services that require the same basic set of activities to produce them. Each value stream is its own business unit, with customer and financial responsibilities. Value streams pay for valued services delivered by Stakeholder and Enterprise Architecture COEs.

The Enterprise Architecture COE is also subservient to value stream COEs, and responsible for assuring organizational, business, application, technology, information, and physical architecture exists to enable organizational capabilities.

Value focused Organizational Structure - Centers of Excellence model

Center of Excellence (COE)	**Future Areas of Concentration** Each COE is responsible for value delivery with positive cash flow. Value Stream COEs purchase value from Organizational COEs	**Traditional Functions** A list of traditional functions / applicable activities to support value stream processes. *Denotes traditionally uncommon functions
Stakeholder Value, Organizational Development & Performance Management	**Organization-wide responsibilities:** Collaboration with Value Stream COEs to ensure all organizational efforts support value delivery • Stakeholder Relationship Management to include Value Stream Leaders. • Brand Management & Communications • Health & Safety • Human Resource Management & Development • Organizational standards for Employees, Suppliers, Partners, Investors, Communities, Societies, Economies, Local and Global Environment and Regulatory Compliance • Performance Management, Process Controls, and Financial Standards	Account Services Business Process Management* Communications Compliance (Safety, Health, Environmental, Financial) Customer Service Finance Human Resources Public Relations Marketing Operational Excellence* Project Management* Project Portfolio Management* Risk Management Strategic Planning* Supply Chain Management Training*

Center of Excellence (COE)	Future Areas of Concentration Each COE is responsible for value delivery with positive cash flow. Value Stream COEs purchase value from Organizational COEs	Traditional Functions A list of traditional functions / applicable activities to support value stream processes. *Denotes traditionally uncommon functions
Value Streams End-to-end core value delivery processes grouped by families of product / service offerings	Value Stream Center of Excellence responsibilities: Served by Organization-wide COEs • Product / Service Development • Product Promotion • Customer Acquisition • End-to-end value stream product / service delivery and performance management • Product Servicing • COE Specific Customer, Employee & Supplier Experience	In order of value delivery process: 1. Research & Development 2. Product / Service Design 3. Product / Service Management 4. Marketing 5. Sales 6. Operations 7. Quality Assurance 8. Field Services 9. Product / Service Distribution 10. Customer Service

Center of Excellence (COE)	Future Areas of Concentration Each COE is responsible for value delivery with positive cash flow. Value Stream COEs purchase value from Organizational COEs	Traditional Functions A list of traditional functions / applicable activities to support value stream processes. *Denotes traditionally uncommon functions
Enterprise Architecture: Organizational, Business, Application, Information, Technology & Physical Architecture.	Organization-wide responsibilities: Collaboration with Value Stream and Stakeholder COEs to ensure process health • Physical and Technology Asset Management • Application Portfolio Management • Information and Knowledge Management • Technology & Physical Infrastructure • Cyber & Physical Security	Asset Management Enterprise Architecture* Information Technology Knowledge Management* Real Estate Management Risk Management Security

Each COE is responsible for its financial success. Value stream COEs pay for services provided by the remaining COEs in the organization. Now for the formation of each COE starting with identifying value streams.

Identify Value Streams

With defined value propositions, you can begin identifying value streams – end-to-end processes that deliver on these promises. Below are some values stream examples by industry to guide you. Each Value Stream produces goods and services that are similar in nature, with each major activity in a value stream being a value stage.

General Value Measurement Guidance:

It is imperative that at every value stage, or at multiple activities in a value stage, that you are measuring how well the core and sub processes in the COE are performing in delivering value. This allows for controlled calibration and improvement – preferably measuring in real-time or in the smallest time lags possible. In other words, there should be feedback loops at every value stage to ensure strong process performance communication to everyone involved in value delivery. Local and overall Value stream performance measures can be cycle time (time to complete an activity or value stage), quality (% correct the first time), on-time delivery, time to equipment maintenance, overall lead time, stakeholder experience, and any compliance or industry specific measurements.

Services Value Streams by Service Family
1. Service Design
2. Service Promotion
3. Customer Acquisition
4. Service Delivery
5. Customer Value Experience

Value Measurements: Value Stream performance for Service value delivery, Customer, Employee and Supplier experience

Manufacturing / Software Development Value Stages by Product Family
1. Product research & development / Requirements gathering
2. Product Design / Prototype
3. Product Promotion
4. Customer Acquisition
5. In house or Supply Chain Product Manufacture / Software Development
6. Assembly / Unit Testing
7. Test / Regression Testing / User Acceptance Testing
8. Product Distribution
9. Field / Technical Support
10. Customer Value Experience

Value Measurements: Value Stream performance for Product value delivery, Customer, Employee and Supplier experience

Healthcare Value Streams
Population Health Management by Population served
1. Identify Population Health & Well-being Trends
2. Proactive Health and Well-being Management
3. Population Health Measures
4. Population Sampling – Experience
5. Pay for value model – no health insurance needed
6. Accountability measures for positively promoting the health and well-being of individuals and populations.

Value Measurements: Value Stream performance for Population Health & Well-being value delivery, Customer, Employee, Provider, and supplier experience

Temporary Illness, Emergent/Urgent, Surgical, Behavioral Health, Chronic Disease Management)
1. Patient presents with issue/illness/injury
2. Perform value health services to treat illness/injury
3. Accountability for Treatment Effectiveness / Quality of Life Improvement measures
4. Patient and Provider Experience
5. Life and Health Insurance offered by the same provider to drive accountability

Value Measurements: Value Stream performance for Treatment Effectiveness / Quality of Life Improvement value delivery, Lead Time, Customer, Employee, Provider, and Supplier experience

Education for Children
1. Identify meaningful groups of talents and capabilities for growth and development with the goal of children being happy and productive members of society

2. Develop programs based on groupings of talents and capabilities
3. Identify each child's innate talents and capabilities
4. Deliver three-dimensional hands-on environments and practices to groups of children based on the talents and developmental capabilities with those groups
5. Each child progresses at their own rate
6. Measure Child, Parent, and Educator experience
7. Measure societal impact

Value Measurements: Value Stream performance for Child Development by talents and capabilities, Child, Educator and Parent experience, Child Capability and Talent Maturity Progression

Lifelong Ongoing Education Value Streams by Capabilities

1. Program Development, Change Management, and Retirement
2. Program Promotion
3. Instructor / Coach & Student Onboarding
4. Program Delivery
5. Support and Measurement of Student Progress
6. Maturity model by areas of development
7. Life-long learning success measures

Value Measurements: Program Value Delivery, Student, Employee and Instructor / Coach Experience, Maturity model efficacy, Life-long learning progression

Government / Public Services

For government / public services, each would follow the basic Services model. The question to ask is: what programs and services are value-added to the population governed vs. in place as political bureaucracy? We want to identify value outcomes for the governed public and streamline the process of delivering this value at the local or federal level.

These models may challenge current societal practices, but they are all value focused on the individuals or populations served. Now, how do we determine the leaders in a value stream centric organization?

Centers of Excellence (COE) Leaders

"The less the company needs you, the better off it is."

– Jack Wu

Each COE interacts with all other COEs to ensure that best practice adoption occurs in all value streams or organization-wide processes where applicable. It is important to share new and improved ways of working to adopt in similar processes and activities within the organization. The focus is on delivering value, not on one area performing better than another. Share the knowledge, share the wealth.

Value Stream COE Leaders

Each value stream will require a leader, someone accountable with their teams for the health of the entire value stream. Unlike traditional situations, value stream leaders have complete end-to-end visibility into how well a value stream is performing. A master business process engineer is a great partner for a value stream leader and depending on the size and complexity of the value stream, you may need more business process engineers to support the design and continuous improvement of the value stream. This includes where other processes supply or interface with the rest of the organization. Master BPEs should regularly facilitate strategic planning and provide valuable facilitation of the design or structure of a COE to best support the value streams and supporting processes.

Value Stream COE leaders need to have a clear fundamental understanding of the entire process, and good process measures will help with understanding how well the current processes work. The COE leader and sub-process managers ensure that everyone has the necessary tools and is prepared to work in the process. Incentivize teams working for maintaining and improving process health and that they consider connected processes when devising improvements. Here it is imperative that teams become self-directed, and that these teams can take empowered action within the boundaries agreed upon – which would include process control. This assures that quick fixing is no longer a practice, but instead that only proven sustainable solutions for improvements prevail.

Stakeholder Value, Organizational Development & Performance Management COE Leader

This leader is accountable for defining and assuring the overall value that the organization delivers to stakeholder groups met. For each value stream there are a myriad of support processes necessary for value stream health and this role is accountable for driving meaningful communication and standard practices across various areas of the organization. Standardization of process performance measurement and the management of stakeholder relationships is a critical focus for this COE.

This COE measures entire organizational performance and holds leaders accountable for overall organizational health, designing balanced metrics that drive the right behavior inside the organization to assure value delivery to all stakeholders.

This COE coordinated standardization of processes and this leader should work with other COE leaders to lead the standardization of employee roles and responsibilities and that incentives are fair across the organization based on the responsibilities of any given role. Also coordinated by this COE are general internal and all external communications for the organization. All communications related to organizational and process changes should start with defining the opportunity or problem with a why – why the change is happening, and the data to back up the need for the change. This type of thorough communication assures everyone in the organization understands the reasoning for, and has the knowledge to apply, the changes necessary to adapt to shifts in stakeholder value definitions.

Enterprise Architecture COE Leader

This leader is the Enterprise Architect (EA) of the organization and is to embrace all areas of enterprise architecture. The enterprise architecture model has six architectural components: Organizational, Business, Information, Application, Physical, and Technological. The classical enterprise architecture model of today is purely technology focused, as the technology profession invented it, yet cannot agree upon the model. The enterprise architecture model that I propose encompasses developing and supporting all structure (tangible and intangible / technological / non-technological) that an organization requires to function in enabling value streams .

---

ar·chi·tect (ärkə‚tekt)

noun: a person who designs structures and, in many cases, also supervises their construction

synonyms: designer, planner

verb: design and make

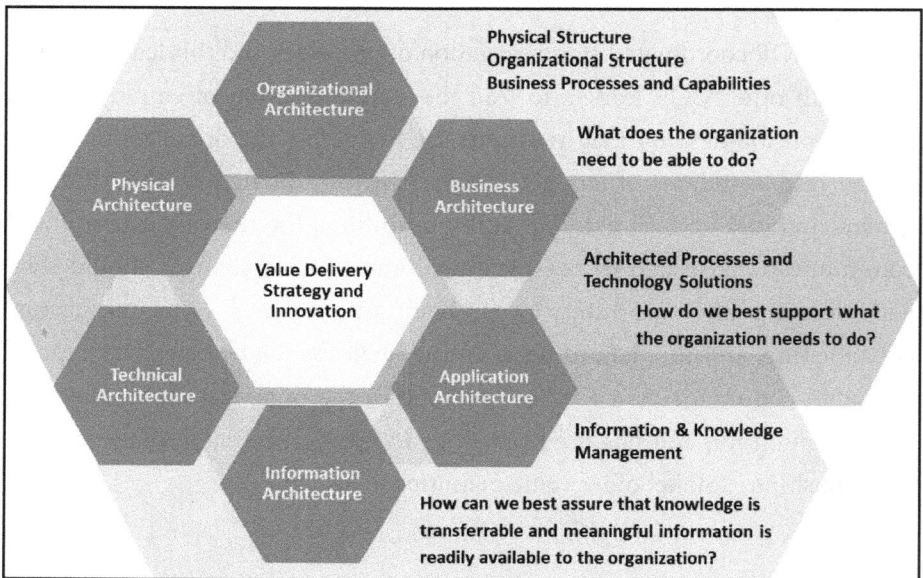

Six Enterprise Architectures

We need to understand what the organization needs to be capable of to deliver value. Defining the business capabilities influences process and technology design.

A capability is a set of tasks that a person or system is potentially able to perform at a certain performance level.

Adapted from https://www.dragon1.com/terms/capability-definition

---

The leader of the Enterprise Architecture COE is not necessarily to be a traditional technology leader, or even a technology expert at all, even though a substantial portion of the accountability of this COE is based in technology. Traditionally, technology leaders have failed to see the importance of process in creating practical technology that will enable an organization to deliver value. Early in my career I was under the impression that technology-focused individuals thought like engineers, but generally they do not. Instead, "techies" tend to be either

- creative types that, given too much artistic license will take vague requirements and creatively solve for those requirements in a way that may not provide the value necessary for organizational success, or
- incredibly detailed thinkers that may drill into details while missing the big picture goal.

It is rare to find technology leaders that have the joint talents of big picture thinking, the ability to communicate in laymen's terms, understand the importance of process and standards, and that enjoy nurturing relationships with people. This COE leader needs to be able to develop with other organizational leaders, the strategies, and the structures necessary for the best allocation of tangible and intangible resources to maximize the potential of delivering value to stakeholders and in doing so, this leader must support the integrity of each value stream.

Rigid and slow-moving models no longer cut it. The challenge is to move toward a structure that is agile, flexible, and increasingly collaborative while keeping the rest of the business running smoothly. Successful incumbents become agile by simplifying.

They let structure follow strategy and align the organization around their customer goals with a focus on fast, project-based structures owned by working groups making up different sets of expertise, from research to marketing to finance.

*While companies often obsess about the "boxes and lines" of organizational structure, it is more important—and significantly more difficult—**to focus on processes and capabilities.***

https://www.mckinsey.com/business-functions/organization/our-insights/six-building-blocks-for-creating-a-high-performing-digital-enterprise#

I mostly agree with the assessment above but take exception to the statement "significantly more difficult to focus on processes and capabilities." In the traditional world, yes, but not in The Future of Working Together Model, where organizational transformation and performance sustainability can be quite straightforward.

Aligning People and Technology to Organizational Processes

Each process needs to be able – to be capable - of delivering value to another process or to stakeholders. For people, to be able to do something means you are capable. Align people with natural and learned capabilities to the correct sequence of activities in any given process that requires that set of capabilities. When activities are dangerous, repetitive, tedious, or complicated for humans to enjoy performing, or where human error is far more likely, Technology may enable those activities.

The following practices aim at supporting COE leaders in better understanding their roles and empower individuals to take on new innovative ways of working. Our value-focused structure will drive new behaviors ending the need for traditional practices to prevail.

The Future of Working Together Practice #5: Promote all Types of Diversity

---

Replaces the traditional practice of failing to promote all types of diversity

---

Bringing together people of differing ability helps teams innovate and expand the limits of ideas and solutions. Someone with a marketing background may contribute to improving an engineering design. People become overly familiar with their area of expertise and when others that are not familiar with that way of thinking are involved, we experience innovative magic. In our new value delivery focused structure, everyone aligns to, and is responsible for, supporting value delivery and therefore cross-functional collaboration *naturally* becomes a normal practice. What has been missing in traditional organizations is the appreciation that one area of expertise can contribute to another. Involving all types of functional experts that exist in your organization in the design and control of the value delivery system is paramount, along with keeping the pulse on new marketplace innovative disruptions and trends to sustain the organization.

The Future of Working Together Practice #6: Powerful Communication

---

Replaces the traditional practice of positive spin communication

---

"To effectively communicate, we must realize that we are all different in the way we perceive the world and use this understanding as a guide to our communication with others."

- Tony Robbins

With everyone accountable for the health of a value stream, there is freedom to call out what is not working as well as to suggest improvements to processes, structure, technology, environments, and the organization overall. In a value-focused organization, leaders need not be the expert that tries to solve organizational problems in a vacuum, but instead empower everyone and create a culture of ownership and pride.

When utilizing The Future of Working Together Model it is much easier to promote a culture of curiosity and collaboration. In the context of powerful communication, there is no such thing as negative or positive information – only meaningful data and opportunity. Incentivize people to do what is right for the long-term viability of delivering value. No one person is more important than another as everyone has a valuable contribution to offer. Organizational cultures that have been traditionally more passive-aggressive tend to be cultures where people fear to speak up. As an example, I find healthcare environments to be highly passive-aggressive as traditionally it has not been a team-based culture, but a doctor tells nurse culture. Healthcare organizations are a double-edged sword – the organization is hierarchal and so is the care delivery model – creating more opportunities for missed communication and weak value delivery than other industries.

An Instant Message between me and a colleague:

Me: There is such a blame culture in healthcare! The biggest opportunity is to have people realize that it is a poorly designed process that allows for mistakes. Most errors come from process complexity, not from people trying to do a bad job. The number one corrective action taken in healthcare is to blame and retrain. Do not blame people, blame the process! Processes have no feelings! Processes do not mind if you work to improve them.

Colleague: I am stealing "processes have no feelings" ©

Me: ☺

In the new model, it is disadvantageous to make another team member look bad. Encourage everyone to speak the truth about what is working and not working, and if a sensitive matter arises, people must be willing to have face-to-face constructive conversations with the person that can make the difference. Gossiping about others is intolerable - a coward's game. In a value-focused and value delivery structured environment, it is much easier to encourage everyone's participation and have all ideas heard. Celebrating team collaboration and success is the key to creating a Wildly Successful Enterprise.

The Future of Working Together Practice #7: Measure Process Performance

---

Replaces the traditional practice of subjective employee performance reviews

---

"The greatest waste is failure to use the abilities of people."
– W. Edwards Deming

If you want to have high performing employees, have them feel valued. People want to contribute to the success of the organization and are often not in the position to do so in traditional organizations. Creating viable processes allows people to bring their innate talents and do their best work. With well-engineered processes, the people working to enable those processes know what adds value and what does not, and if they are not adding value, this behavior immediately becomes clear. The extreme minority of people that do not want to work to improve process health will either learn to collaborate from peer pressure (everyone else is collaborating), leave to pursue other interests, or asked to leave the organization.

In a value focused environment, the need for employee oversight should be minimal.

The Future of Working Together Practice #8: True Leadership

Replaces the traditional practice of Politics, Nepotism and Favoritism

---

"The manager accepts the status quo; the leader challenges it."
— Warren Bennie

"Leadership is deciding where we will go and build, Management is building it."
- Aidan McCullen

To lead effectively, it is imperative to question the status quo. In the traditional model, organizational leaders are functional experts that have proven to excel in that area of expertise, assumed to also be good leaders or managers. Leadership and Management roles are ill-defined in the traditional model. Here we will define these roles and show how new organizational structure based on value delivery allows people with innate talents in leadership and management to flourish.

Leadership *is a function of direction setting, aligning constituencies, and being motivating and inspiring.*

Management *is planning, organizing, staffing, process control, and problem solving.*

Adapted from Lean Leadership: A Model for the New Millennium

Future Leaders

"Our leaders are different than they were just six years ago. We are no longer leading through command and control. Leadership is about finding joy in serving others. Leadership is not a right; it is a gift and today, more so than ever, we must earn the privilege to lead."

- CEO Mehran Assadi, National Life Group

Leaders are people who can bring teams together for a common cause. Leaders are visible and approachable, concerned for employee welfare, are effective time managers, and do not intervene as a problem-solver, but enable others to do so. Leaders empower others to do remarkable things. Leaders subordinate their ambitions and egos to the goals of the group or organization. They must be capable of having a sense of humor, generating vision, extraordinary motivators, and be effective meeting facilitators.

By comparing traditional and process-centric leadership roles, the dysfunction of leadership in traditional organizations becomes clear. Compare the practices of traditional "leadership" to those of The Future of Working Together leaders.

Traditional Leader Attributes
Individually develops plans
Sets goals
Produces metrics
Enforces rules and regulations
Controls information
Sole problem solver
Functional expert
Assigner of work
Performance appraiser

The Future of Working Together Leader Attributes
Long-term future-focused

Supports teams to set goals and supplies resources necessary to improve outcomes
Is a model of self-accountability
Makes information readily available
Facilitates process focus and health
Leads by example – empowers others
Enables process health
Is accountable with teams for performance
Adapted from Lean Leadership: A Model for the New Millennium.

Leaders do not force outcomes through people, but instead empowers people in aligning to a cause.

Future managers

In The Future of Working Together Model, Managers administrate activities in an organization and provide guidance to those working a process – ideally, they are skilled at assuring an environment where people and process can thrive. Traditional managers focus on people productivity, assigning tasks and projects, managing budgets, and approving timecards. Creating a high-performing team is a rarity in traditional management.

In a value stream structured organization, a manager owns an entire value stream sub-process, not a function. **The process becomes the primary engagement, and the process manager role is to assure the necessary resources are available and coordinated to deliver value.** We want to design any process in such a way that people know what to do and when and how to do it. Allow the workforce to recommend how the process needs improving by designing and measuring the process so that it is obvious to detect where opportunities lie. Within a well-engineered process, it is easy to find who works well in the process and who does not. Here again you will want to engage business process engineers to design powerful processes – with process accountability health measures.

In a traditional organization, where the process is difficult to see and navigate, traditional managers evaluate people performance without consideration of the barriers in the process. A typical performance evaluation is usually based on "did you do what I told you to do?" The focus is usually not on enabling people to grow and develop and to contribute to the organization in the most meaningful ways. Once you have a healthy, measurable, and visible process, it is clear whether someone is aligning with delivering value or not. Peer pressure typically takes care of the rest. **Always blame the process first!** Processes have no feelings and are easy to improve. We have no right to evaluate performance of people that are handed a poor process. Evaluate process performance! Everyone is accountable to improve value delivery through powerful processes.

Managers should ensure that people are cross trained for other roles and that people periodically move to work other areas of the process. This practice helps with bringing new eyes to different areas of the process to uncover opportunities and helps with assuring that no matter who comes and who goes, the process will remain healthy.

Strong Leader Weak Manager	Strong Leader Strong Manager
Too Few in Supply. Strategies lack the support of formal planning.	A rare breed in short supply and considered "true" leader type.
Weak Leader Weak Manager	**Weak Leader Strong Manager**
Found to be in excess and damaging to morale and empowerment.	Bureaucracy and over-specialization has overrun most organizational processes.

Traditional organizations are a breeding ground for weak leaders and managers
Excerpt from Lean Leadership...A Model for the New Millennium (The eighth in a 9-part series on Lean Enterprise and the tools and techniques employed to affect change) by Patrick Lucansky, Robert Burke, and Larissa Potapchuk.

What a wonderful experience we can create for everyone by focusing on delivering value to our stakeholders involved compared to the demoralizing management practices in traditional organizations!

The Future of Working Together Practice #9: Measure Value

Replaces the traditional practice of measuring what we can

"Improve quality, you automatically improve productivity."
— W. Edwards Deming

The premise of this book is that of organizational transformation followed by the **pursuit of continuous improvement - the ongoing process of making controlled step-change improvements**. Apply the practices in this book to transform your organization into one that will be future-ready and then continuously innovate and improve to adapt as the future requires. You have to measure in order to improve anything. How can you improve what you do not measure?

Many people say they want to lose weight – but what they really want is to lose fat and gain or maintain muscle mass. You can measure your weight loss with a weigh scale, but the weigh scale will tell you nothing about WHAT percentage of what component – fat or muscle – that you have gained or lost.

Ensure enough detail so that measures can accurately portray how well a process is performing in delivering intended outcomes. With good measurement comes good decision-making. Defining stakeholder value includes how to measure value creation. You can create value and still not be working efficiently. To create good quality the first time (vs. correcting product and service problems downstream) you want to measure value delivery by creating measures for quality of work supplied to and along the value stream. It is paramount to understand your organizational processes to the level that you can measure quality along the way to value delivery and determine how well you are able to produce quality outcomes the first time. Measuring quality will allow teams to predict outcomes prior to delivery of products or services to customers and help determine what to adjust with the process to ensure quality. Every process should have controls to best ensure that processes remain healthy and reliable.

Balance of measurement is vital - you get what you measure. If you measure only speed or productivity without measuring quality, you can produce poor quality products and services delivered at the rate desired. If you measure only money, you have no idea about quality, speed, or satisfaction. So be careful what you measure!

To create a high performing organization means to create high performing teams. Balance measurements of quality and satisfaction will over time improve speed and financials. Focus on the quality side of the equation and the value will be there – quality of products and services and quality of experience for stakeholders.

You may have heard of balanced scorecards – these are combinations of metrics that best depict a balanced approach to value delivery of an organization. I have developed many balanced scorecards for various organizations, and these were usually the first of their kind. Balanced scorecards pave the way for balanced measurement. You do want a balance of measurements for your COEs and your organization and be prudent in the choice of your metrics – as what you measure drives behavior. Assure all metrics are well defined and that everyone understands we are aiming not to "hit" numbers, but to continuously improve overall value.

The Future of Working Together Practice #10: Organize Once

Replaces the traditional practice of reorganization into similar top-down functionally based hierarchies

---

"Unless companies change these rules, any superficial reorganizations they perform will be no more effective than dusting the furniture in Pompeii."

– Dr. Michael Hammer

Ideally, we would design an organization from its start to be value delivery focused, just as an expert gardener prunes a tree from the time it is a sapling. However, it is possible to re-design existing organizations by engineering high-performing yet flexible processes, re-aligning people to capabilities of those processes, and defining the technology necessary to automate steps that are dangerous, repetitive, tedious, or complicated.

Structuring your organization to deliver value need only occur once. As you add new products and services, they will either align with a current family of products and services in a value stream or become a new value stream.

Value-focused structure promotes diversity of thought, innovation, efficiency, speed to market, and adaptability for any organization. Now to keep what you have gained we need to make our third paradigm shift from point-fixing to an overall value delivery process health mindset.

Chapter 10
Future Mindset

"I should estimate that in my experience most troubles and most possibilities for improvement add up to proportions something like this: 94% belongs to the system [common cause] (responsibility of management) and 6% special [cause]."

– W. Edwards Deming

The future of working together mindset to take on is that of systems thinking. Operational Excellence (OpEx) is a system-thinking approach. The fundamental problem in trying to implement OpEx principles is that you are superimposing a system on a traditional organizational structure that naturally rejects systems. Additionally, most of the population does not naturally think in terms of systems. I will not promote Operational Excellence here as it exists in the traditional sense. There are organizations that have some form of OpEx efforts in play, most of which are not embracing the right mindset to have those efforts be fruitful and/or sustainable. My own profession has failed to recognize the paradigms we have traditionally lived in, and no amount of process improvement or instruction of these methods will transform an organization that has the wrong Focus, Structure, and Mindset, as the organization will tend to unravel the improvements made.

Our new mindset begins by understanding Value Stream Analysis as a practice for the design and improvement of processes. When performing value stream analysis, I will find **most opportunities in the process gaps that**

exist either between departments or from disparate technologies, but in our new value-focused structure these issues naturally dissipate. Forming a value delivery process-centric structure creates an environment that can now properly support OpEx concepts as well as other practices, and this is why I address structure before mindset. The mindset of your organization needs to be an improvement of traditional OpEx approaches by applying the fourteen proven practices covered in Part 2 of this book. I directly address OpEx practices in two of the fifteen practices addressed in this book, and I have infused other OpEx concepts at the right time throughout the book.

What I have taken on in Part 2 of this book is to capture fundamental practices you need adapt to create a Wildly Successful Enterprise. Some practices may sound familiar, but the context or approach may differ from what you may have learned or experienced during your professional career.

Forget About Setting Goals. Focus on This Instead.

Prevailing wisdom claims that the best way to achieve what we want in life is to set specific, actionable goals.

Eventually, I began to realize that my results had little to do with the goals I set and everything to do with the systems I followed.

Forget about setting goals, focus on your systems instead.

If you completely ignored your goals and focused only on your system, would you still succeed?

I think you would.

Adapted from Atomic Habits by James Clear

Systems Thinking

"An ineffective system will beat a good person every time."
– W. Edwards Deming

As someone with innate talent in seeing the workings of organizations as groups of systems and processes, in the past I took for granted that everyone else does as well. Just like our bodies have various systems – cardiopulmonary, digestive, circulatory, endocrine, and so on, so do organizations consist of systems. Examples of the organizational systems are communication, measurement, distribution, production, service delivery, process change management and control, quality management, financial, mechanical, workforce management and information systems to name a few.

You live and work in systems every day. A traffic system is a fitting example of a system that you have become unconsciously competent at navigating. How often do you realize that you just drove somewhere, preoccupied with other thoughts most of the journey? Your brain navigated the system unconsciously. When you first learn to drive, you learn the standard system. It is a simple system incorporating visual clues that you learn and then easily navigate in, and you did not have to design it to follow the system.

The way traditional organizations work would be analogous to every department having its own piece of a traffic system that it can change at any time. One department owns the traffic lights and decides to change the colors of the lights, or the order of the light sequences. Another department has responsibility for the lines on roadways and decides to change the colors and patterns to their liking. How well would traffic systems work if this were the case? Anyone can adopt a system quickly if it is well designed, and traditional organizations tend to have weak systems as any systems that are in existence are by chance and/or take tremendous oversight to sustain. One system commonplace in organizations is the compliance / regulatory system, which is usually its own department superimposing requirements on top of a chaotic structure.

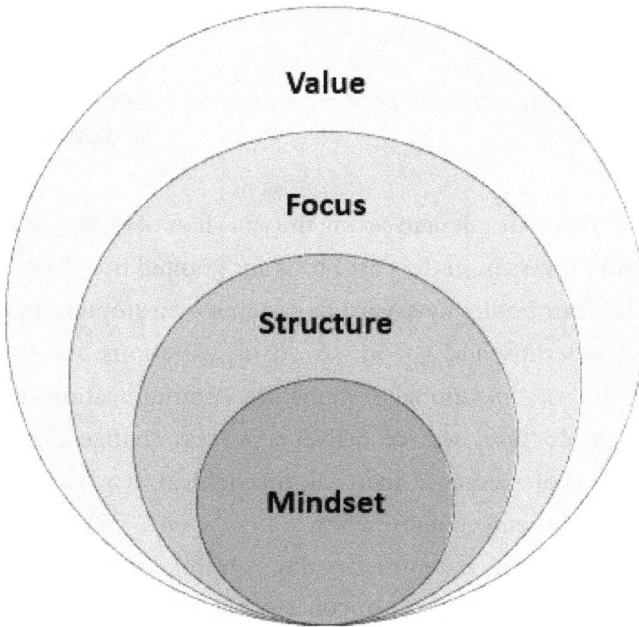

The Future of Working Together – An Organizational Systems Model

To cultivate a powerful organization, it is best to define the systems that need to exist in the organization. There will be systems that already exist, yet since these systems grew organically, they will need review and attention, transformation, or elimination. If you perform an internet search on organizational systems, you will find a diverse multitude of organizational systems models, and I have found few that are close to being easily adaptable and that these models promote the traditional paradigm, therefore they are overly complex and ineffective. There is power in simplicity.

I estimated before starting this book that ten percent of the population were natural system thinkers – those who perceive the world as a conglomeration of interacting systems. Upon performing research on the subject, it turns out that my estimates are fairly accurate. Yet, anyone can apply systems thinking, and systems thinking can become culturized easily as The Future of Working Together Model pulls for pragmatic systems and structures. Systems thinking comes so naturally to me that I realized while authoring this book that there is a need to define systems thinking for the general audience.

When first outlining this book, I made a list of what I thought were key attributes or ways of thinking that take advantage of systems and processes. Once my list was complete, I researched to see if I could discover what I may have left out simply because I take it for granted. I was happy to see most of what I had compiled aligned with a study I discovered titled *A New Path to Understanding Systems Thinking* by Nalini Linder & Jeffrey Frakes:

The tools and skills of systems thinking are not always consistent with the way people naturally think, compared to becoming fluent in a foreign language. It takes time and repetition to build skills and confidence in application.

... even with repeated exposure, some individuals consistently disregard most systems thinking practices, dismissing their value or return on investment.

In contrast, some individuals quickly embrace discovering the "language" of systems thinking and say: "This is the way I've always thought; you're just giving me language to express it."

Michael Goodman, "Systems Thinking as a Language," The Systems Thinker, V2N3

David Bridgeland, "Technology Versus Discipline: Why I Am Not a Systems Thinker," The Systems Thinker, V9N2

In The Future of Working Together Model it is easier to understand, adopt, and follow the system than to stick with tradition. The following is a good list of systems thinking attributes and some explanation as to why, for most people, systems thinking is not a natural way to perceive the world. But, just like the traffic system, anyone can become unconsciously competent in navigating and contributing to the maturity of organizational systems – the system just needs to be well-engineered.

17 Systems Thinking Practices
1. **Considering both short- and long-term consequences of one's actions:** *Looking ahead and anticipating not only immediate results but also future effects.*

2. *Looking at multiple perspectives of an issue:* Changing perspective to see other points of view within a system.

3. *Looking at the 'big picture':* Focusing on the overall 'forest' as opposed to the details of any 'tree'.

4. *Looking for patterns in data:* Reviewing information with an eye towards patterns or themes.

5. *Looking for trends over time:* Viewing changes over time as part of the natural dynamics of the system.

6. *Being comfortable with ambiguity:* Holding the tension of paradox and ambiguity; taking the time necessary to understand the dynamics of a system before acting.

7. *Checking results and changing actions if needed:* Assessing for improvement using benchmarks; seeing errors to learn and adjust.

8. *Looking for interconnected issues:* Perceiving connections between multiple issues/parts within a system.

9. *Looking for small actions that can make big differences:* Using systems understanding to determine what small actions could produce high leverage results.

10. *Considering the impacts of accumulations over time:* Paying attention to things that build up (or deplete) slowly over time—both concrete ('money in a bank account') or abstract ('trust within a relationship').

11. *Being comfortable with questioning one's deep assumptions:* Understanding that one's beliefs of how the world works (mental models) may limit one's thinking.

12. *Understanding that boundaries are arbitrary.* Checking for consistency of understanding about a particular boundary.

13. *Thinking critically about causation, not just correlation:* Looking beyond basic connectedness to understand the dynamic relationship between the connected parts.

14. *Being cautious of adopting a win/lose attitude:* Being skeptical of a 'zero-sum game' approach to individual goals within a highly interdependent system.

15. *Considering unintended consequences:* Anticipating ancillary effects of actions over time.

16. *Seeing self as part of system under study:* Understanding that one's own behavior within the system, impacts the system.

*17. **Recognizing that a system's structure drives its behavior:** Focusing on system structure and avoiding blaming others when things go wrong.*

Next is an added excerpt from the *A New Path to Understanding Systems Thinking* study that depicts a new way to focus on system adaptation by the workforce as a principal structure of an organization. In this study they take the 17 Practices of Systems Thinking listed above and apply Myers-Briggs Type Indicators™ (MBTI) to correlate behavioral preferences with systems thinking.

We engaged in a study to see if at the individual level, a link might exist between a person's personality and his or her preference for using systems thinking skills using two main activities:

1. We developed a comprehensive inventory and administered a survey of practices commonly associated with systems thinking.

2. We compared assessment responses to participants' MBTI typologies.

Note: We chose the MBTI based on its popularity, name recognition, and the possibility of comparing our data to other MBTI correlation studies.

The four MBTI dimensions:

*- **Extroversion (E) or Introversion (I)**, relating to how individuals focus their perception on the world around them. E's gather information by exploring the world around them and I's tend to focus inward.*

*- **Sensing (S) or Intuitive (N)**, relating to a preference to focus on basic information you take in (S) or interpret and add meaning (N).*

*- **Thinking (T) or Feeling (F)**, relating to making decisions. T individuals prefer to first look at logic and consistency as opposed to F, who first look at the people and special circumstances.*

*- **Judging (J) or Perceiving (P)**, relating to how one deals with the outside world. J individuals like to have things decided whereas P tend to prefer to stay open to new information and options.*

Statistically significant preferences for 17 Systems Thinking Practices by MBTI Dimension

	17 Systems Thinking Practices	**E/I**	**S/N**	**T/F**	**J/P**
1	*Consider short-and long-term consequences of one's actions*		N		
2	*Looking at multiple perspectives of an issue*		N		P
3	*Looking at the "big picture"*	E	N	F	P
4	*Looking for patterns in data*		N		P
5	*Looking for trends over time*		N		
6	*Being comfortable with ambiguity*		N		P
7	*Checking results for lessons*		N	F	
8	*Looking for interconnected issues*		N		
9	*Looking for small actions that make big differences*		N		
10	*Considering the impacts of accumulations over time*				
11	*Being comfortable with questioning one's deep assumptions*		N		
12	*Understanding that boundaries are arbitrary*				
13	*Thinking critically about causation, not just correlation*				
14	*Being cautious of adopting a win/lose attitude*		N		P
15	*Considering unintended consquences*				
16	*Seeing self as part of system under study*			F	
17	*Recognizing a system's structure drives its behavior*		N		P

Note: all p < .05. Letter denotes a statistically significant difference amoung the respondents for the dimension preference.

---

*The findings from the overall analysis suggest that within the general population, **some segment of people naturally practice and prefer systems thinking as a way for them to better understand complex issues.** This tendency is not necessarily related to someone's capability of applying a given systems thinking practice or its frequency of use.*

Adapted from https://thesystemsthinker.com/%EF%BB%BFa-new-path-to-understanding-systems-thinking/

Interestingly, the N – Intuitive and P – Perceiver type naturally think in terms of systems. This is of no surprise to me personally as my MBTI is ENTP, with ENTP being a MBTI type that represents only three percent of the population. This enforces my recognition that I see the world as a collection of interconnected systems and patterns and that my thinking is quite different as compared to most people. One could conclude that non-systems thinkers are not naturally inclined to design an organization to perform as well as a systems thinker – but that does not mean that they cannot adopt systems – people do it every day.

Another interesting fact is that the tools recommended for enhancing systems thinking practices in the article above referenced *process engineering methods and tools*, correlating with my professional training and experience aimed to improve organizational performance. No matter the Myers-Briggs Indicator Type of a team participant, the methods, and tools that BPEs practice *allow for everyone to easily take part in systems thinking* and for teams to make objective decisions based on fact, not opinion. It is critical to long-lasting success in designing any organization to involve people that do not naturally perceive the world as groups of systems to collaborate using these methods and tools. Utilizing non-biased methods and tools can help with identifying and designing each organizational system, which will in turn identify the cultural behaviors necessary for success.

Systems thinking is fundamentally different from that of traditional business thinking. Traditionally the focus is on managing people within a functional area. In contrast, systems thinking encompasses understanding all the interactions that produce the behaviors or results in a system. The future of working together practices use systems thinking with objectivity so that teams learn how to use systems thinking to their advantage.

A business process engineer wrote to me: Everybody wants to do it their way, but if 10,000 people tried to design a freeway the way they wanted to, we would not have any infrastructure.

There must be a balance where we have enough rules to keep order while at the same time new ideas entertained. Typically, people performing the value work are not listened to; they are feeling the pain of the design of the organization yet cannot effect positive change.

It breaks my heart, and I work like crazy to fix it with solid process changes that will alleviate some of the nonsense, but it is barely a tap into the problematic system.

Traditional operational excellence (OpEx) efforts have focused on operational efficiency and problem solving and usually found to be in play in manufacturing - and even more specifically in the operations / production departments. What OpEx does not address is that the CEO and leadership teams are traditionally balance sheet focused and do not understand the importance of process while ignoring the organization structure needed for operational excellence.

After aligning organizational focus and structure to stakeholder value, then we can take on the mindset of true Operational Excellence. What OpEx typically does not address is the condition of process, people, and technology architecture of the organization (Practice 13) nor the exorbitant amounts of resources traditionally wasted on unproven projects in motion across the organization (Practice 14).

The Future of Working Together Practice #11: Problem-solving and Prevention Mindset

---

Replaces the traditional practice of rewarding quick fixes

"Manage the cause, not the result."
– W. Edwards Deming

There are many proven problem-solving methods in existence and here I will not choose one method over another, nor supply detailed education of how-to problem solve. Most traditional organizations do not formerly apply proven problem-solving methods as a practice. If you are not using a proven problem-solving method, you are not aware of the root cause of the problem and therefore will not prevent future related issues.

What is most important to understand is by simply following the guidance provided in this book you can prevent traditionally common organizational and business problems from ever occurring. Engineer processes to prevent problems, as good process design mitigates issues with value delivery. There are proven methods that best ensure you design your product or service for best value, and I recommend using them.

For any problem-solving effort, it is imperative to create a safe space where people can speak truth and drive collaboration through data, not opinion. In The Future of Working Together Model, consider potential breakdowns or failures that could occur in your value delivery process, products, and services, and design the causes of these potential breakdowns or failures out of a process, product, or service before you implement it. Your products and services, and the processes that produce them, can be well-designed with a value focus, thereby mitigating customer issues before they can happen.

When designing a process, people usually focus on what is the "happy path." They focus on how they want the process to go, and do not consider designing the process to also consider potential failures that could occur in the process. OpEx practitioners use tools such as Failure Modes and Effects Analysis (FMEA) to "break" a potential process, or product or service design, on paper to assure a robust design. We want to determine what could happen that could cause a process, product, or service to fail to deliver value, and either design out the possibility of that failure occurring or design the process or product or service to address the issue when it happens.

Prevention is the goal of root cause analysis; when unforeseen problems do occur, we need to identify and eliminate the cause of the problem. For free guides to problem-solving and robust product / service design, please visit wildlysuccessfulenterprises.com.

The Future of Working Together Practice #12: Developing Powerful Solutions

---

Replaces the traditional practice of "Brainstorming"

"You are either part of the solution or you are part of the problem."
– Eldridge Cleaver

"If I had one hour to save the world, I would spend fifty-five minutes defining the problem and only five minutes finding the solution.
"– Albert Einstein

A common behavior that develops in traditional organizations is to work to quickly solve the effects of problems. We instinctively start solving a perceived problem as we encounter one. It is common, that as I observe people working (with the goal of determining where the hidden problems lie within processes), that as these people will show me an issue with the process and suggest what they perceive is a better way to work the process. I usually have to ask several why questions to get them to the root of the problem. It is not normal for people to consider what is really causing the issues that affect them in completing their work as intended, as in a traditional organization they have little to no awareness of upstream activities that cause the issue. Rarely has anyone ever asked me what I might think is causing the issue they are experiencing and instead they will offer a change to the process that they believe will eliminate the negative effect they experience. People tend to offer solutions, instead of questioning what caused the problem in the first place.

Healthcare Providers are Health Insurance Stakeholders – Part 2

Recall my prior example (Chapter 8) of a health insurance company Provider Call Center working to reduce call transfers as a solution to increased budget expenses.

*The increased cost was an **effect,** or outcome, of problems within the value delivery processes worked elsewhere in the company. Yet the solution was to reduce call transfers.*

Instead of collaborating with other areas of the business to improve value delivery processes that caused the problems, and therefore caused increased volumes of problem calls, the department focused internally on the negative effects to their budget and had determined the problem was with their call flow design!

Calls received in the center were typically related to Healthcare Providers needing the insurance company to correct a problem with the timing or disposition of a medical procedure review or an error in claim processing – actions elsewhere in the company that had taken place several days, weeks, or months prior to receiving the call.

Having identified at least one billion dollars of waste in the medical review and claims processing processes in the company at that time, I recommended to leadership that we work to improve those processes to ensure timely and accurate outcomes. These leaders had no interest in taking on that endeavor due to politics.

The Focus, Structure, and Mindset of the company influenced people to stick to the myopic approach of creating localized solutions to mitigate the effects of upstream process issues.

The problem they focused on was increased costs and their solution was to reduce call transfers. There was no attempt to get to the root cause of the problem and create a viable solution – improving the value delivery process design.

The traditional customer service model can do nothing more than placate customers and is a latent reaction to problems generated either from weak value delivery processes or product and service designs. There is no value delivered in solving problems that should never have happened in the first place. Customer service centers do not have the influence to address another departments failure to deliver value. Traditional organizational focus and structure make it difficult to determine the root cause of a problem and the traditional mindset is to create a solution to mitigate the localized effect of a problem occurring elsewhere. Often we quickly schedule a "brainstorming" meeting to solve an ill-defined problem.

Do we want instead to actually be creating powerful solutions to the real problems at hand? There are two areas of interest relating to the development of powerful solutions.

1. Powerful process solutions
2. Powerful product or service design solutions.

The proven practice of Brainstorming is one of many methods available to create powerful solutions, but first you must understand what problem you are solving. Brainstorming is a tool included in the overall best practice approach to process or product and service design and improvement.

The Brainstorming Method

The method of Brainstorming is a solution generation tool used as one step during the problem-solving process and can be helpful when developing new products and services. To Brainstorm, you begin with understanding what stakeholders value and develop solutions to deliver that value.

How to apply Brainstorming as a method:

1. **Request a BPE to facilitate** process or product / service design improvements.
2. **Form a team**. The team should be comprised of people working the process where the negative effect is experienced, as well as people working the upstream processes that feed the process where the negative effect is experienced. The makeup of this team assures diversity of thought and expertise, representing every critical activity that contributes to the process. It is best to include all stakeholders that experience the outcome of the process or use of the product or service, so include downstream internal and external stakeholders and customers.
3. **Define and quantify the problem.** Any proven problem-solving method will help the team with defining the problem. Walking the real process, versus discussing how we think the process works, is typically the only way to find out what is failing.
4. **Perform root cause analysis to uncover one or more causes of failure.** From this activity we identify opportunities for improvement. Applying Process Engineering or Product / Service Engineering Design techniques will reduce or eliminate all occurrences of the cause(s) of the problem. If not all causes per preventable with good process engineering, solution generation (brainstorming) is a viable option.
5. **Perform Brainstorming as needed.** Facilitating a brainstorming session (idea contributions from the team) assures all participants can offer innovative ways to determine the cause of and then to solve the problem. Record all ideas, assuring a safe space where people can freely offer ideas, no matter how absurd ideas may seem to other members of the team and without negative comment. One idea offered by one participant can trigger a brilliant idea in another participant's mind.
6. **Use data to prioritize a list of potential solutions.** A Priority Matrix is a great BPE tool for accomplishing this to assure objectivity.
7. **Test the viability of the highest priority solutions.** There are BPE methods for statistical testing of solutions to determine the best solution to utilize.

8. Implement the best solution.

9. Measure the ongoing viability of the solution as well as overall value delivery.

There are many idea generation methods available, brainstorming is only one method.

For free guides to creating powerful solutions to problems or for products and services, please visit wildlysuccessfulenterprises.com

---

The Future of Working Together Practice #13: Business Process Management (BPM)

Replaces the traditional practice of Implementing Technology to fix process issues

---

"Instead of embedding outdated processes in silicon and software, we should obliterate old processes and start over."
– Dr. Michael Hammer

"The first rule of any technology used in a business is that automation applied to an efficient operation will magnify the efficiency. The second is that automation applied to an inefficient operation will magnify the inefficiency."
– Bill Gates

Business Process Management (BPM) is a discipline involving any combination of modeling, measurement, optimization, execution, control, and automation of business activity flows in support of enterprise goals spanning systems, employees, customers, and partners within and beyond the enterprise boundaries.

Adapted from BPM.com

With a new organizational focus and structure, we now nurture a process-centric and continuous improvement mindset. BPM is a process management system to best ensure that every process in the organization is well defined, measured, and optimized while also understanding how processes interact. BPM is a method inventorying all processes in a standard notation, known as Business Process Management Notation (BPMN), to allow for the modelling of processes to maximize performance. BPM can aid in choosing the best technology to invest in.

Estimates are that Fortune 500 companies alone lose half a trillion dollars annually from process inefficiencies. What if your organization could reduce operational expenses by just 5% and re-invest that money into necessary infrastructure? To start, begin by mapping your organization at the highest level - mapping all core and major support process. This will help guide better process designs at a more detailed level. Create and link the inventory of processes using process modeling software to determine where bottlenecks and inefficiencies occur. BPM also contributes to best identifying business capabilities across the organization, leading to effective alignment of people and technology to process.

Today, most development of information systems happens without adequate process analysis. Automation can be an expensive way to lock in an underperforming process for a long time. Traditional technology implementation projects do not include measuring the efficacy of the solution implemented, driving needing to create workarounds while waiting for additional technology enhancements to replace them at added cost. It is not unusual to launch a partially developed technology solution due to cost overruns from lack of process design, so workarounds end up becoming permanent, with the organization now further overburdened with ineffective and inefficient processes. It is uncommon to never fully complete the implementation of technology solutions and for leaders to not appreciate the impact.

Spending the time up front to design robust processes before even choosing the technology to enable them will deliver best value with improved ease of use and functionality at a much lower cost. In utilizing BPM within our new organizational model, it is much easier to choose the right technology to enable processes.

Case Study: Merger & Acquisition drives New Technology Development

The Problem:

A healthcare consortium acquires three health coaching organizations with a vision of creating an innovative way to best serve the chronically diseased population. The focus is on creating new technology to perform the analytics to identify cohorts with chronic disease and provide patient service and coaching platforms to help people manage their disease effectively.

The project is behind schedule and trending over budget with systems development already started in India. Six months into the project, leaders are still debating over the design of systems and workflows.

The Chief Quality Officer, also a BPE, knew the team was not following best practice process design approaches and she brought me in to bring the project back on track. On the first morning of the 2-day meeting, I listened to unguided conversations without much resolution or accomplishment. I approached the technology leader at the lunch break and explained how I was confident I could get the team on track. He was frustrated enough to agree to my proposal.

My advice to him was that we needed to slow down to speed up.

	Traditional: Directors presenting PowerPoint decks with the vision for their departments and group brainstorming about systems and workflow solutions	
The Approach		**Business Process Engineering:** *Best Practice Process and Systems Design*
What Happened	*After 6 months of bi-weekly meetings, there was not enough information to develop the detailed requirements to support the vision. Development had already begun on the new system, but requirements ambiguity had already absorbed one third of the project budget.*	Within two days a high level end-to-end measurable process with major system interfaces identified. For two weeks, facilitated teams to develop input/output maps from each department to ensure all process and systems interfaces accounted for and no gaps in design existed.
Business Outcome	*6 months behind schedule and trending to $3M over budget.*	Project completed on time and on budget.

That afternoon I led the team in mapping the vision as a value stream and as someone new to the industry my questions brought out many assumptions, further clarity, and collaboration. By late afternoon, the business leaders had taken over creating the map and I stepped aside and facilitated from the back of the room. They had learned to fish.

When you professionally design a process to include measuring how well it is performing, any automation should improve how the ideal process can work manually. Design technology to monitor performance of the process and have valuable information to properly problem solve and continuously improve. Most organizations have reams of data but little valuable information. Enterprise architects need to partner with business process engineers to ensure that business process management is at the forefront of enterprise architecture.

A note on Value Stream Mapping

"Nature does constant value stream mapping - it's called evolution."
- Carrie Late

To establish the processes in your organization, map the current processes using value stream mapping methods. This method allows the business to streamline the processes prior to performing BPM and allows for the BPM model to be cleaner from the start.

It is through value stream mapping that I have uncovered billions of dollars of opportunity in organizations. You will want to find experts that really know how to use this method.

A note on Quality Management Systems

For those organizations that follow a standard quality system please take heed. Most organizations apply the quality management system over their business rather than embedding the recommended best practices into their processes. Years ago, I co-authored a book "A Field Guide to AS9100" to show how this aerospace quality management system can help make a company better, not just to be compliant to it. Even though the version of the AS9100 standard has changed, the recommendations I made in this book are timeless and The Future of Working Together Model makes it easier to implement those recommendations. Any organization with formal quality systems can benefit from reviewing the recommendations in the book, available at https://amzn. to/3DD6Jbp.

The Future of Working Together Practice #14: Utilize Project Portfolio Management

---

Replaces the traditional practice of assuming infinite resources

---

"All improvement happens project by project and in no other way."
– Joseph Juran

What is a Project Portfolio?

We all have financial portfolios at some level of maturity. You may own real estate, an automobile, a home and/or other tangible assets. You may have an investment retirement account where your hard-earned money is in stock, bonds, and/or mutual funds. You may own stock in a company, have cash savings, and the list goes on. This combination of investments and assets is your financial portfolio. You manage your portfolio of investments; you decide what to invest in, you consider your goals, risk tolerance, and future earning potential. Investments usually serve us for a period, and we hope to obtain our desired outcome from them at a point in the future with greater value than we originally invested.

No one wants to lose when making an investment. We would never buy a home without knowing the real estate market, knowing what features we want in the home, what locations we want; ensuring that our home will deliver on our needs. While supplying shelter and security for your family now, a smart investment will assure your home value will increase over time. You may invest in an improvement project to further increase your home value for your family while you are living there, and for future return on investment.

Any project is an investment, and projects consume resources to produce a desired outcome. Therefore, choose your projects wisely – like you would when buying a home.

Projects are investments – choose them wisely

How does your organization decide what projects to run?

- Are they brainstormed by the leadership team annually during budget season?
- Are there "pet" projects in play– someone's great yet unproven idea?
- Are regulatory mandates top priority, stopping other critical work?
- Does the first solution to a problem become a project?
- Does the organization require upgraded equipment or systems yet the capital and resources for performing this work are consistently not available?

Project Portfolio Management (PPM) is a practice that most leaders are unaware of and therefore is not present in most organizations. In the traditional paradigm, CEOs believe that once goals and objectives are set for functional leaders, that these leaders will take the right actions for the overall business, and we have already established this is not a sound assumption. Allowing functional experts to meet goals however they see fit will drive various uncoordinated projects across the organization, tying up valuable resources without guarantee of solid outcomes. In a traditional setting, leaders believe it is solely their responsibility to solve problems that keep their department from meeting goals, and therefore set in motion various projects based on unproven ideas or that will duplicate or conflict with other efforts outside of their department. Since the organization is not focusing on the most important efforts and assuming infinite resources, people become overwhelmed trying to perform their regular duties (work the process) while supporting multiple projects. If every area is executing unvetted projects to change processes and systems across the company without coordination, then we have no control of what the overall outcome for the organization will be, and we are spending time and money on unnecessary efforts.

Most organizations have a myriad of projects identified or in flight that are not worthy of the resource load it takes to complete them. Whenever I have implemented PPM, after properly vetting all projects that exist in some form, it is not unusual to deny or cancel around 50% of these projects. After ranking the remaining viable projects by relative importance based on overall organizational needs, release projects in order of priority when they can be properly resourced. This assures each project executes quickly and delivers needed results.

We use significant resources on projects – one-time efforts that typically take resources from other operational needs. You want to choose projects that create the highest return – the greatest positive impact with the least effort. Designing healthy processes first will reduce the need for projects to fix issues and allow projects that are necessary to be successful. **The goal is to dramatically reduce the risk of investment for every viable project.**

Benefits of Project Portfolio Management (PPM)

PPM drives the accountability to apply right resources to the right effort at the right time.

1. Prioritize investment in the most positively impactful projects
2. Resources appropriately identified and planned for each project
3. Accelerate project completion and results
4. Increase number of projects completed annually
5. Stakeholder satisfaction improves with progress

Governance

Governance drives accountability across the enterprise to choose the best utilization of resources and assures open communication channels for all project stakeholders. The intent of a governance process is to assure all projects provide a positive return on investment and that the entire project portfolio is viable. Everyone in the organization understands and appreciates, and no one circumvents, the governance process.

A governance committee that represents all areas of the business reviews each project idea submitted to them. I recommend that representatives of the governance group cycle on and off the committee every six months, and not all at once, to assure fairness and objectivity.

Identifying and Selecting Projects

A proven way to identify low effort / high positive impact projects is to value stream map your business. A value stream analysis utilizes real data to uncover hidden, holistic opportunities in your business to solve for inefficiency (engaging in activities not valuable to stakeholders, not flowing value continuously, elimination of workarounds) and ineffectiveness (delays, backlogs, errors, poor quality, poor communication and feedback, poor information flow, weak measurement, compliance issues, stakeholder issues, incongruent technology).

Projects may surface to support non-process related efforts such as a new product design, marketing campaign, or the construction of a building. Regardless of the solution, **every project should have a business case**. A business case quantifies justification for why the project is important and compares this to the level of effort that will be necessary to deliver intended outcomes which in turn determines the level of return on the investment.

Ranking Projects

Utilize a BPE to develop a method for prioritizing projects that considers multiple factors important to the organization. Determining the best combination of factors and weightings usually takes some time to dial in but is well worth the effort. Examples of factors to consider for project alignment to value delivery and organizational viability are:

1. Regulatory compliance (with an example of ranking criteria):

   1 = not urgent (implement within 1 year)

   4 = somewhat urgent (within 6 months)

   7 = urgent (within 3 months)

   10 = extremely urgent (ASAP)

2. Risk tolerance
3. Alignment with one or more business strategies
4. Efficiency Gain
5. Quality Improvement
6. Revenue Gain

Launch projects in order of priority and based on available resources

The top-ranking projects now need to be resourced. Here we assure all necessary resources are available for a project prior to launch. If a top ranked project cannot be fully resourced, you have a few choices. If a project in flight could supply those resources and it now ranks lower than the newly ranked project, you can put a hold on the project inflight and execute the more important project or wait to launch the new project until resources are available. This is not intuitive, as people tend to believe that just working on things is more effective than waiting, but this is also a false belief. **PPM will execute more projects in less time than you ever thought possible when you follow these guidelines,** to include using proven project management practices to facilitate all projects through to completion.

Project Management

Project Management is a best practice that performed well can dramatically improve the time and effort required to complete any vetted and qualified one-time effort. Project management is another highly misunderstood role in most organizations. Just because someone has managed a project, this does not make them a Project Manager. Projects are resource intense efforts led by a qualified project manager – not just a functional manager or subject matter expert. To save resources and time and to deliver the intended outcome, it is worth the investment to use a Certified Project Manager. Program Managers oversee groups of projects. Program and Project Managers need to feel empowered to deliver all the news, good and bad, and our new organizational mindset will support that.

Validate project outcomes as soon as possible

I developed a project plan template early in my career that incorporates all best practices from project management and process engineering. That plan (known as a work breakdown structure or WBS) has activities identified for adequate process analysis and verification of the business case and early validation points built into the project to ensure as soon as possible that deliverables are meeting the intended outcome. Often, I see validation planned only near the end of a project and creates delays with problems discovered too late to execute on time or budget. I have followed this WBS for every project I have led and every project I have led to completion was successful.

Case Study: The Berlin Brandenburg Airport Project €2.5 Billion overrun

---

A significant case study of project failure is Berlin's Brandenburg airport. The airport's feasibility and preplanning phase took 15 years and construction started in 2006, with target opening date October 2011. Nine years late, the Brandenburg Airport opened in 2020, with an estimated total project cost of 7.9 billion euro, well above the approved budget of 5.4 billion euro!

What went wrong?

Project Rationale was ill-defined with wrong purpose and priorities

Project Stakeholders were many with differing interests

Communication breakdowns in declaring project status

Scope Creep with too many additions to the originating project scope

Insufficient Validation to ensure the meeting of standards

The issues mentioned in the case study above are also common to many organizational projects due to lack of governance, lack of the determining and agreeing to the problem and the outcome desired by stakeholders, the lack of following project management best practices, and lack of strong and complete communication channels. Seasoned project managers can only be successful if the environment stands for project integrity, starting with proper planning and scoping. In business, pre-planning should include stakeholder and process analysis – traditionally rarely performed prior to project kickoff.

Chapter 11

The Untapped Experts

> *"Out of one hundred men, ten should not even be there, eighty are just targets, nine are the real fighters, and we are lucky to have them, for they make the battle. Ah, but the one, one is a warrior, and he will bring the others back"*
>
> *- Heraclitus*

Introducing the Business Process Engineer

On any given day, you will hear about executives, doctors, lawyers, politicians, firefighters, police officers, scientists, but rarely engineers. I believe the reason for this is that engineers design systems, processes, products, and technology to work without failure, so engineering goes unnoticed as only negative news sells, and it is rare that a well-engineered process or product fatality occurs.

---

en·gi·neer /enjəˈnir/

*noun: **a person who designs**, builds, or maintains **structures** and/or systems.*

*synonyms: originator, deviser, **designer, architect,** inventor, developer, creator, **mastermind.***

*Verb: **design and build** (a machine or **structure**).*

We take for granted all the infrastructure in place today because we already trust it to not fail. So, what does engineering have to do with business? An engineering mindset is what is missing in the design of organizations as in this mindset we think in terms of workability, structure, fit, form, and function. Even though business process engineering has existed for decades as a practice and profession, the mainstream still either does not utilize, or poorly utilizes, process engineering approaches to improve business structures and processes to accelerate organizational performance.

Following the recommended practices and organizational model in this book can end traditionally common organizational problems and therefore there should be no firefighting to perform. Instead, proactive work can prevail such as designing and improving processes to deliver stakeholder value. Designing workable processes with a focus on maximizing value delivery is what Business Process Engineers do. Most traditional leaders have little idea of how to best utilize BPEs, as traditional leaders work in a 2-dimensional world with focus on managing people and applying technology. Top MBA programs do not teach even the basics of good process design. If a process or operational excellence team exists, it is traditionally not a mainstream function in the organization. The business process engineering profession has also failed itself, as we have historically assumed the mainstream believe processes are important. I used to believe people thought processes were important, too, but I gave up believing that over 10 years ago. By this point in this book, you should have a good understanding and appreciation of the fact that creating healthy business processes is paramount to success. *Processes are the primary conduits to all value delivery.*

Landing on the Hudson

"It took all of us and we did it all together."
— Captain Chesley "Sully" Sullenberger

I tear-up every time I recall US Airways Flight 154, an Airbus A320-214 which after takeoff from New York City's LaGuardia Airport on January 15, 2009, struck a flock of Canada geese just northeast of the George Washington Bridge and consequently lost all power in both engines.

Every process and aircraft part worked that day as designed. *Every safety instruction given to passengers, every crew training, every pilot training hour went into the success of that plane landing on the Hudson River with all lives saved. We design Jet engines to withstand an average flock of birds, but not the flock that crossed the flight path that day. Nonetheless, the pilot had prior water landing training, and the plane engineered to float upon a successful water landing for a long enough period to allow the crew to execute long-practiced maneuvers to sustain passengers and crew until help arrived.*

In the aerospace industry,

- Processes ensure the highest benefit from people and technology.

- People trained and certified to execute processes with checks and balances that ensure these processes are adhered to. For example, in aerospace the training of production and field mechanics, flight attendants, pilots, and air traffic controllers on carefully designed processes is consistent. Even travelers receive training on every flight "should there be a drop in the cabin pressure…"

- Systems designed to withstand far more than necessary to reduce the chance of failure, and back up systems exist for flight critical systems.

- Technology pursued to improve performance, including low weight/ high strength alloys and composites, casting, forging, balancing, finishing, testing, of turbine blades and the like. All three dimensions – Process, People and Technology - support successful flight, which is the same approach that put a man on the moon.

The aerospace industry continuously improves in all three dimensions to ensure that new processes, people, and technologies continuously improve for reliability. Any failure in this industry, unlike healthcare, educational and government systems, society holds the aerospace industry accountable to learn from every failure.

I recall contacting my former comrades in aerospace quality assurance that day to celebrate. "Everything we work hard to enforce everyday – it all worked!" I exclaimed as tears streamed down my face. And yes, every carefully engineered system and process came together that fateful day to make a win.

Make note that the movie made about this flight titled "Sully" has the focus being entirely on the pilot. Hollywood must sensationalize a hero and our society pulls for experts over process. Make no mistake, an execution of a series of well-designed processes occurred on that day. The movie focuses on pilot ability and downplays all the systems, processes and all the other players that made that landing work. We do want expert pilots at the helm of an airplane, no doubt! ***Systems and processes are not sexy in our society, but they could be if people understood they are at the cornerstone of us surviving.***

Systems, processes, people, and technology – all of it - made that flight successful, including the training Sully received over his career – which had him avoid failure - to make the right call that day and land on the Hudson. He knew his crew and all the other systems and processes in place would take care of the rest..

Many factors contributed to everyone surviving the emergency landing on that fateful day, and Sully is first to admit it - the mindset of true leadership.

Organizations Engineered for High Performance

As within any profession, you need to have talent essential to the role. Traditionally, training of BPEs on process improvement methodologies is the norm. Not all BPE's are versed in Project Management, Change Management, BPM or PPM. Some are method purists and incredibly detailed thinkers, and they are not the ones to help to design your entire organization as proposed in this book.

To be an exceptional business process engineer is to bring neutrality to a situation while applying the right teaming, change management, and process improvement methods at the right time to skillfully lead teams through new territories of creative thought – all necessary and traditionally divergent talents. To appreciate what engineering an organization can look like, it is important to understand how engineers think.

Engineers...

Pay attention to how things work.

Visualize framework.

Pay attention to what things are used for.

Visualize things in three-dimensional space.

Learn how simple mechanisms work.

Do the math.

Think of how to improve things by finding ways to increase limits.

Think of tasks that need accomplishing.

Stay up to date with technological innovation.

Look to nature. Nature has evolved into the most robust, simplest, and most direct designs.

Analyze the structures of things.

Adapted from http://www.wikihow.com/Think-Like-an-Engineer

It is clear that not just anyone can fulfill a BPE role. We all have our own innate talents to bring to society, and while drafting this book it became clear to me why the engineering profession is underutilized.

A former Master BPE colleague of mine once stated:

"We have always been in the crosshairs. We challenge tradition and

limits; we aim for new possibility. It shakes peoples' very foundation of how to run an organization."

In a traditionally designed and operated organization, yes, we are always in the crosshairs.

We BPEs have lived a most exhausting role, given by the very nature of the traditional paradigm. We cannot go it alone; we need functional experts to partner with us on what they need to do to perform a specialty as we guide them in *improving how the process or system can work*. It takes all of us to create a new future of working together. **Business Process Engineers do not make the business work, we help make the business work better.**

To produce this book, I had to consider everything I learned over the years, but even more importantly, I needed to assess *why* I learned what I did. Had I not experienced the frustration of repeated resistance and layoffs, I would never have asked the questions that led to me discovering the traditional paradigm.

The Foundation of Business Process Engineering

In existence for close to one hundred years, business process engineering concepts have surprisingly low adoption, and we have by now proven why; living inside the traditional paradigm has us assume functional experts can design effective cross-functional processes. The development of quality and cost-effective manufacturing practices as the industrial revolution took flight was a contribution of several key players, including Henry Ford, Edward D. Deming, and Joseph M. Juran. Phillip Crosby joined the crusade a few decades later and Michael Hammer a couple of decades after him. They pioneered business process re-engineering and efficient manufacturing and quality control. These and many other experts have proven, demonstrated, and written about countless ways to improve organizational performance – creating higher value for all involved at lower cost. Due to these breakthrough concepts, airplanes fly today at a stellar safety record, medical devices supply life-saving technology, everyday products perform without a hitch. Unfortunately, there lacks good translation for some process engineering concepts for service industries, and some BPEs struggle with adapting to intangible service environments.

Business process engineering efforts have many titles such as Total Quality Management, Lean Six Sigma, Business Transformation, Continuous Improvement, Process Excellence, Performance Excellence and Operational Excellence. These approaches and methodologies are function and industry agnostic in bringing proven ways for people and organizations to create outstanding results. What I am speaking to here is total organizational transformation, with a scope far beyond process improvement.

The founders of continuous improvement methods created structures and practices to train others. Some process improvement practitioners have embraced these practices so diligently they have lost sight of the big opportunities with organizations. Simply training individuals in a traditional organization on Lean Six Sigma is ineffective, as the organization does not appreciate process and will not create an environment to embrace this advanced skill. *Pragmatic in my approach, when I am engaged to improve organizational performance, I first set out to identify and evaluate an organizations core process while implementing Project Portfolio Management to free up resources to optimize process performance.*

Many of my peers still believe that improving any process in an organization makes a difference. And improving a process will have influence, but only for the short term, as the organization will eventually unravel the process. Traditional organizations cannot sustain process improvement gains by the very nature of their Focus, Structure, and Mindset. Process improvements unravel in a 2-dimensional world, as a traditional organization does not measure and control its end-to-end value delivery processes. And before process, it is the systems in an organization that need addressed.

The automotive industry now produces vehicles to perform far more reliably than in the past, with "the average age of cars on the road in the US reaching an all-time high of 11.4 years, which is a full 3 years longer than the average age of cars in 1995."[1]

The reason? The implementation of systems that can reliably deliver higher quality at lower cost.

[1]http://www.aei.org/publication/5-charts-showing-theres-never-been-a-better-time-for-average-americans-to-own-operate-a-car-the-good-old-days-are-now/

To engineer reliable products and services involves advanced methods in design as well as process improvement and control. There is low adoption of these practices in service and transactional industries and in administrative areas. I can say most in my profession have failed to apply concepts derived originally in manufacturing to service and transactional environments. I moved into healthcare from aerospace over 15 years ago and have easily adapted to service and transactional, healthcare, educational, and software development environments.

BPEs become certified to assure adequate understanding to a body of knowledge and application, like many other professions. A BPE receives training, and unfortunately only some receive mentoring, on the improvement of business processes by applying various methodologies, objective team facilitation, data driven decision making, and project and change management practices. Continuous improvement methods work because they drive objective improvement and decision making vs. the subjective decision making that occurs in traditional organizations.

BPEs perform analysis of business processes and how people and technology work within those processes. BPEs create efficient and effective processes and measure what matters to *keep the process flexible yet in control. Process control means knowing the process is always delivering your organizations value proposition – it does not mean lack of flexibility.* BPE's are data analysts and change management leaders. Proficient BPE have mastered these capabilities and deliver outstanding results. A neutral and objective party with passion and vision, a strong BPE can plan large efforts, communicate at all levels of the organization, transfer knowledge, and lead teams large and small. Expert process engineers can train and mentor to grow and develop others into the field. Few BPEs naturally function as organizational designers.

BPEs facilitate the development of strategies with leaders, lead large teams to realize new futures, and given copious amounts of data can statistically prove what is working and not working. They dig into the process details to figure out why problems within the company exist. They can design best practice measurement systems, enhance quality and compliance, and lead an organization for the first time to manage their project portfolio wisely on time and on budget. A qualified BPE will consistently find opportunities that will pay for the cost of employing them several times over, year after year. Ironically, conventional wisdom has CFOs downsizing or completely eliminating the process engineering team whenever a budget cut is considered a solution to inefficiency and ineffectiveness of an organization.

The Organizational Designer

Professionally, I have outgrown even the multi-talented role of BPE, and title myself an Organizational Designer or Business Transformation Expert. Unfortunately, business transformation is ill-defined in the world and there are many companies whose leaders think they are transforming their organization and yet are not. This book delivers a model for complete business transformation. Having studied, practiced, and enhanced my abilities for over two decades as a business transformation expert, applying design and engineering concepts and process focus, *I first view the entire organizational landscape to start transformation from the top-down.*

To design your organization to flourish you will need to engage someone with this multi-faceted background to design the organization for greatest performance by following The Future of Working Together Model. Additionally, use one or more seasoned BPEs for every value stream (depending on size and complexity) to collaborate with teams to continuously improve those processes to reach optimal performance while staying in tune with technology disruption and customer trends changing over time.

I developed the Wildly Successful Enterprises Program^{SM} to affordably coach everyone in the organization through transformation – to take a journey together from status quo to being a Wildly Successful Enterprise. To find out more, visit wildlysuccessfulenterprises.com.

A Note on Innovation

The most important effort you can make to accelerate innovation in your organization is to adopt The Future of Working Together Model with the Focus, Structure and Mindset I have proposed in this book. This will create an environment for innovation, and innovative practices will be much easier to instill. Now your organizational focus, structure and mindset can assure you deliver value. The advantages of setting up these three pillars allow organizations to be adaptable, innovative, scalable, effective, and profitable. Most importantly, you will offer an environment where the people working in the organization can supply real value, be joyful, and thrive.

Know what to do

> *"It is not enough to do your best; you must know what to do, and then do your best."*
>
> *- W. Edwards Deming*

Every organization has a purpose to deliver some form of value to society, yet organizations are misaligned to the very purpose for which they came into existence in the first place. How we organize ourselves in business is bankrupting the workforce and consequently society. When you think about it, we do not consciously design organizations, we simply arrange people into a hierarchy of experts which opposes a focus on method and process. Method is key to sustainable value delivery.

Processes are at the core of everything we produce, and therefore, a value stream process-centric organizational model is timeless. To truly win, it all boils down to how we design our organizations.

Therein lies the answer, and the beginning of a new era.

Chapter 12

The Future of Working Together Organizational Model

"Improvement usually means doing something that we have never done before."

- Shigeo Shingo

"There is a need for chaos and order. Too much order and you fossilize. Too much chaos and you fall apart. These things are always in fruitful harmony."

- Dr Iain McGilchrist

Be Wildly Successful

The Wildly Successful Enterprises Program^{SM} is the **ONLY** business transformation program designed to end **ALL** common organizational problems - quickly and simply as compared to other transformational programs.

Status quo business practices create problems. There is a better way.

DIFFERENT does not mean DIFFICULT

I developed the Wildly Successful Enterprises Program to support leaders in quickly evolving the Focus, Structure, and Mindset of their entire organization, leading to unprecedented results in all areas of organizational performance. This is what is possible when we can embrace a powerful Future of Working Together. For more information visit wildlysuccessfulenterprises.com.

Comparison Table of Traditional Practices to The Future of Working Together Practices

	Part 1 – Traditional Practices		Part 2 – The Future of Working Together
Ch 2	Traditional Focus	Ch 8	Future Focus
1	Budget Control	1	Process Control
2	Downsizing	2	Always the Right Size
3	Hidden Costs of Mergers and Acquisitions	3	Merging Process, Technology and Culture
4	Arbitrary Goals and Bonuses	4	Accountability
Ch 3	Traditional Organizational Structure	Ch 9	Future Organizational Structure
5	Not Promoting All Types of Diversity	5	Promote All Types of Diversity
6	Positive-spin Communication	6	Powerful Communication
7	Measure Employee Performance	7	Measure Process Performance
8	Politics, Nepotism & Favoritism	8	True Leadership
9	Measuring What You Can	9	Measure Value
10	Reorganization	10	Organize Once
Ch 4	Traditional Mindset	Ch 10	Future Mindset
11	Rewarding Quick Fixes	11	Problem-solving and Prevention
12	Brainstorming	12	Developing Powerful Solutions
13	Implementing Technology to Fix Problems	13	Business Process Management (BPM)
14	Perpetual Projects & Assuming Infinite Resources	14	Project Portfolio Management (PPM)

The Future of Working Together Model - Design and Implementation Plan

Listed below are the primary steps to take to create and sustain a Wildly Successful Enterprise. The CEOs new role is to be a leader - to empower employees to focus on supplying value to all stakeholders. The most critical system for a CEO to manage is to incentivize and hold everyone in the organization accountable to creating powerful value delivery processes and outcomes.

Step 1: Focus on delivering stakeholder value

1. Choose to focus on delivering value to all organizational stakeholders.
2. Define your organization's value proposition(s) with stakeholders.
3. Prove your value proposition(s) to be valid and measurable.
4. Ensure everyone associated within your organization understands, appreciates, and aligns to the value proposition(s).
5. Decide how to measure the delivery of value to each stakeholder group. What will a valuable experience look like? How will you know your processes are delivering that value? These measures should be a balance of stakeholder experience, process health and alignment to value delivery, and should be statistically based.

Step 2: Structure the organization for value delivery

1. Master Business Process Engineers are directly involved with every product and process design, and all process improvement activity in the organization.
2. Group your products and services into families. These families of products and services should require similar activities to create and deliver them.
3. For each product family, name your core value delivery process or value stream, and structurally create centers of excellence for each.

- Value streams are the end-to-end processes that *directly* deliver products and services.
- Value streams are groupings of related products or services that have many common elements of activity.

4. 5. Assign a Leader to each value stream. This leader needs to be a leader as defined in The Future of Working Together Practice #8: True Leadership. A value stream leader does not need to be a functional expert for every, or any, aspect of value creation. This leader is accountable to empowering teams serving and working within the value stream in delivering value to stakeholders.

5. Assure the design of processes for best value delivery with real-time measures for process health and stakeholder experience. Value Stream leaders need to understand the value creation process and partner with business process engineers to ensure

- The value stream is well-engineered to deliver stakeholder value
- Measurement of the value stream allows for continuous improvement, problem solving and prevention, and innovation.
- financial and regulatory requirements considered in process design (vs. applied on top of the process).
- Empower people working in the value stream with the understanding that they are responsible, and incentivized, for continuously improving the value stream in a controlled and measured manner.

6. dentify the capabilities necessary to enable the value stream and align people who, and technology that, can perform those capabilities.

7. Measure value stream performance.

8. Establish financial independence for each value stream, as well as incentives for all employees to focus on value delivery. Focus on delivering value and you cannot help but be profitable if your organizational value proposition is sound.

9. For all areas of the organization, recognize the repetitive activities in the

process that technology can automate, simplify, or make safer, faster, or more precise and design that technology for process flexibility.

10. Align organizational COEs and their processes to enable value streams.
11. Every old process is in question, so measure to decide what processes really matter to enable the value streams and design enabling processes to do just that.

Step 3: Develop a Mindset of Accountability and Continuous Improvement

1. Create self-managed teams that assure all resources serve value-added process capabilities.
2. Everyone in the organization is accountable for value stream success.
3. Start with the organization working as manually as possible while perfecting process value delivery.
4. Technology needs to serve the process, not dictate it. Technology should make measurement of the process easy.
5. Measure and improve the value your organization is delivering. Use statistically sound data to make decisions.
6. Problems should be well-defined and quantified, and any effort put towards changing anything in the organization should have a sound business case before finding a solution.
7. Solutions chosen for implementation should have the largest impact (positive gains) with the lowest effort (least number of resources needed to design, implement, and work the solution).
8. BPM and PPM will help with prioritizing projects and activities across the organization.
9. Measure everything necessary to keep your processes, people, and technology healthy in real time. Financial forecasting, budgeting, or other projection analysis becomes either mostly or entirely obsolete.

Which organization would you want to work in?

TRADITIONAL ORGANIZATION & PRACTICES

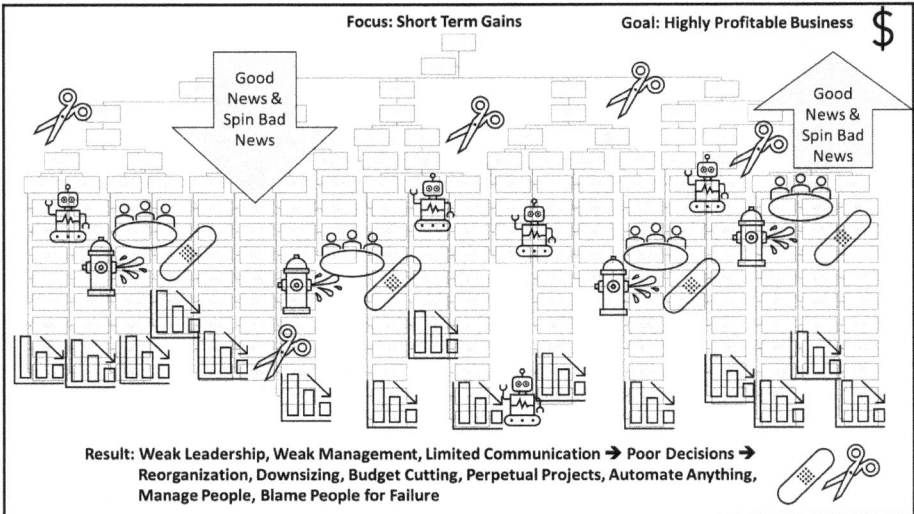

 Fire-fighting – reacting to problems with quick, unproven solutions

 Management by committee

 Band-aid solutions

 Automate whatever we can!

 The numbers do not look good, we need to downsize

 The numbers do not look good, we need to budget cut

VALUE FOCUSED ORGANIZATION

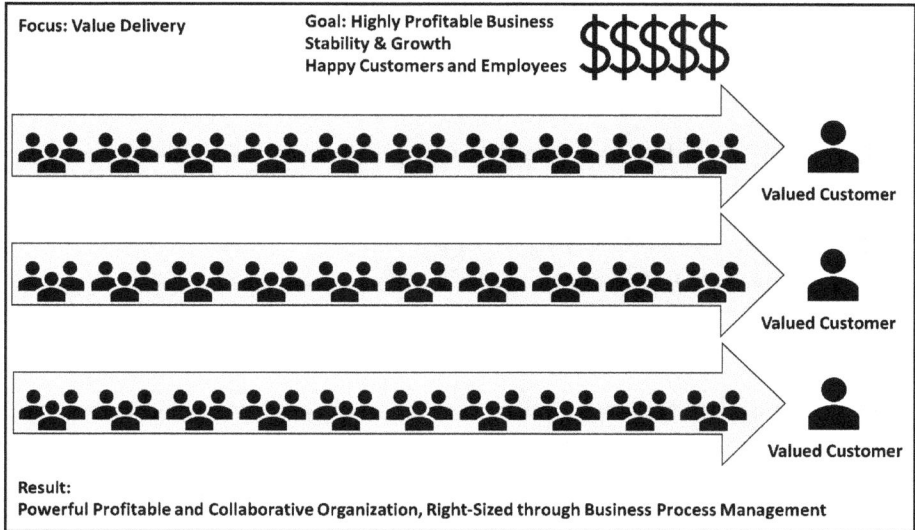

A Note on Resistance to Change

"It is not necessary to change. Survival is not mandatory."
- W. Edwards Deming

"The only thing that is constant is change."
— Heraclitus

"Everyone thinks of changing the world, but no one thinks of changing himself."
– Leo Tolstoy

I often hear people dismiss resistance by saying "people resist change." I do not believe that people *always* resist change. Some people embrace change more easily than others simply because they do not need to know if something works to try it. Fear of change is proportional to the level of control we want in our lives. To not change is a way to control our experience, even if our experience is not what we would like it to be. But like it or not, our world is constantly changing. We naturally resist what feels threatening, confusing, or of no value. We simply do not appreciate innovative approaches if we believe those approaches will not further our pleasure or end our pain, The problem to date with the slow rate of adoption to innovative disruption is that innovations are difficult to imagine being helpful when applied to traditional environments. The Future of Working Together Model creates an environment for innovation adoption and organizational adaptability.

Basic physics tells us that the greater the mass and speed of an object, the harder it is to change its momentum. For those leading small and mid-market companies, you have a smaller mass but a larger speed as your organization grows. As you grow you will take on more mass and grow into stagnation if you continue to follow traditional practices. For those leading large corporations, your organization is oversized, and you will need to embrace what I propose in this book, or your organization will continue to be less and less effective in value delivery. In my professional opinion, most large traditional organizations will not survive the next 5 years without transformation.

By 2027, estimates predict that 75% of the current S&P 500 companies will fall off the portfolio primarily due to disruptive innovation.[1]

Seventy percent of organizational transformations fail due to internal resistance to change.[2]

1 Adapted from "Meeting the innovation imperative: "How large defenders can go on the attack" McKinsey.

---

2 Adapted from "Why do most transformations fail? A conversation with Harry Robinson" McKinsey 2019.

No one is powerless to bring change. My hope is that you will bring the positive change that I propose in this book to your organization and that you share these concepts with the world.

Status quo business practices are nothing but unquestioned evolution.

Until now.

About the Author

Fulfilling on many blue-collar roles and several engineering internships in the energy industry in her native Canada prior to completion of her engineering degree at age 30, Dawn Holly started out with the opportunity to work as an engineer for one of the premier aerospace companies developing Total Quality and Six Sigma as their improvement platform. A natural systems thinker, she quickly became responsible, with four other leaders, for transformational global supply chain initiatives with significant impact. She became certified as a Lean Six Sigma Black Belt in 1999 and taking the role of Master Black Belt in 2005. At that time, she set out to reduce the negative impact to people affected by the complexity of healthcare.

Dawn Holly formed 3D Value Group in 2016 and throughout her career has consulted across every major industry in all sizes of organizations - from startups to Fortune 100 companies - using her many years of experience to generate higher organizational performance with an impact of over $5.2 Billion in revenue generation and over $1 Billion in operational savings through focusing on value delivery and improved stakeholder experience.

Dawn Holly began to write What CEOs Need to Know in 2016 after her eighth career layoff occurring one week after her divorce. During those trying times, she chose to bring positive change to the world. She is the creator of the

Wildly Successful Enterprises Program, designed to transform organizations quickly and simply from traditionally underperforming and non-collaborative into Wildly Successful Enterprises: creating purposeful, productive, and profitable organizations that are joyful to work in.

Dawn Holly lives in Scottsdale, Arizona, has three amazing adult daughters, and enjoys the outdoors and world travel.

Share The Future of Working Together!

What would The Future of Working Together look like for you, your family, and society?

Help me create a world where people and organizations work and contribute to their maximum potential. A world where no human being on the planet goes without their basic needs met – food, clothing, shelter, livelihood.

Here is how you make the world a place where you, and the people you care about, are wildly successful!

Write an amazing five-star review wherever you bought this book.

Ask your local bookstore to stock What CEOs Need to Know. This helps us get more inspiration into your professional circles.

Take the Wildly Successful Enterprises 3-minute assessment to see how close your organization is to reaching its maximum potential at wildlysuccessfulenterprises.com.

Participate in the Wildly Successful Enterprises Program to have your organization reach its maximum potential.

- Rediscover your organizations' purpose and realign everyone in your organization to deliver on that purpose
- Create an environment where people can naturally contribute their innate talents, collaborate, and thrive. Discover how the classical business models do not work and design your organization to outperform the status quo.
- Take on a new mindset or innovation and adaptability for scalable growth and continuous improvement.

To start, visit wildlysuccessfulenterprises.com.

Purchase a copy of What CEOs Need to Know for everybody on your team at dawnhollyjohnson.com. Purchase a copy of What CEOs Need to Know for every leader you know so that they can apply the timeless, purposeful, productive, and profitable organizational model in this book.

Invite me as a keynote speaker to your next event, where I will help audiences recognize three steps they can take today to unleash the potential in their organizations.

Follow me, or 3D Value Group, on social platforms YouTube, LinkedIn, Facebook. Share your insights on social media. This is how other future-focused leaders will find you. We are strong on our own... but we are even stronger together!

We can create a new future of working together!

Your success is my success,

Dawn Holly Johnson

"Dawn Holly Johnson is handing you the keys to the kingdom. If you are ready to ditch "that's how we have always done it" this is the book for you. This is a must read for all leaders looking for a holistic, inclusive solution to meet the demands of today's marketplace. In this book, she clearly reveals the new thinking necessary to create an effective organizational model where collaborative cultures can naturally occur across an enterprise be it big, small or anywhere in between."

 - Jeremy Gustafson, CEO Viking Strategy & Coaching, Master Certified Leadership Coach

"This book focuses on the root cause of why organizations inherit so many inefficiencies and shows how we traditionally just work on symptoms of problems."

 – Jessan Hurkes, Operational Excellence Consultant

"In this exceptionally well-written book, Dawn Holly Johnson uses her vast experience in performance improvement and organizational design to prove that every organization is underperforming compared to its potential. Total company alignment of focus and structure towards value creation will unlock tremendous potential in your business while also creating powerful cultural transformation. I have personally experienced the benefits of value focused organizational structure. This book is a must-read for every CEO and business leader."

– Greg Miller, Managing Director, Alliance of CEOs

"If you hold the top spot in your company, Dawn Holly Johnson's new book, "What CEOs Need to Know" is a MUST READ. Her approach will help you align your team around what matters most. It's time to stop using outdated management models and embrace the future of visionary leadership and collaboration."

- Brandon Barnum, CEO, HOA.com

"This book is excellent! Dawn knows her stuff!"

- Rikia Saddy, Strategic Advisor to CEOs, CMO for global expansion

"You've made a believer out of me! I am so impressed by how well this organizational model works! As we bring on new offerings, we design the process FIRST and test before implementing. This has saved our company and our clients time and money and has enabled the scaling up of our organization. Now, we slow down to speed up and the value is unparalleled."

- Michael Bonanno, Chairman and CEO, Virtual Support Solutions

"Being Wildly Successful takes grit, grace, and gravitas. This book will challenge you to be courageous, lead with generosity and earn trust by rethinking what you know, becoming curious to the core, and re-creating an enterprise that values people, processes, performance, purpose, and profits... all critical and interdependent variables for success."

- Dr. Jackie Freiberg, International Bestselling Author of NUTS!, CAUSE!, BOCHY BALL and more, Keynote Speaker, Coach & Certified Dare to Lead™ Facilitator EpicWorkEpicLife.com